Wonders

CALIFORNIA Content Reader

B

The **McGraw-Hill** Companies

 Macmillan/McGraw-Hill

Published by Macmillan/McGraw-Hill, of McGraw-Hill Education, a division of The McGraw-Hill Companies, Inc., Two Penn Plaza, New York, New York 10121.

Printed in the United States of America

10 WEB 14 13

Contents

California Science Standards

Contents

California
History/Social
Science
Standards

Circuits

A flow of electrical charges is known as an **electric current**. Electric current keeps charges moving, like water flowing in a river or a stream.

To make an electric current, you need a path to carry the current. The path along which electric current flows is called a **circuit** (SUR•kit). A simple circuit has three basic parts. It has a power source, such as a battery. This powers a load, such as a lamp or a computer. Connectors, such as wires, carry electrical charges between the power source and the load.

Many circuits have a switch. A switch turns electric current on and off. The lights in your classroom are controlled by a switch.

To keep charges moving, the circuit cannot have any breaks. A complete, unbroken circuit is called a closed circuit. If the circuit has any breaks or openings, it is called an open circuit. Electric current cannot flow in an open circuit.

When a light bulb burns out, it makes an open circuit. This happens because a wire inside the bulb breaks in two. The circuit no longer has a complete path, so electric current cannot flow through it.

Electric current provides the power that lights up Los Angeles at night.

Picture a one-way circular road. All the cars on this road travel in the same direction in a line. This is how a series circuit works. In a **series circuit**, all the electrical charges flow in the same direction along a single path.

The parts of a series circuit are connected in one loop. The electric current moves along one path. The current moves from the power source through the wires to one load. Then it moves through another load. Finally the current returns through a wire to the power source.

A **parallel circuit** is a circuit in which the electric current flows through more than one path. These different paths are often called branches. The branches of a parallel circuit divide the electric current between them. Some of the electric current flows through one branch, some flows through another branch.

Series Circuit

In a series circuit, the parts are connected like links in a chain. The electric current passes through each part one at a time. If one part of a series circuit is removed or broken, electric current cannot flow through the circuit. ▶

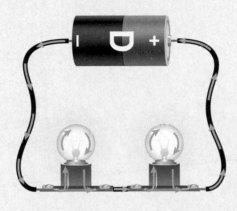

Parallel Circuit

In a parallel circuit each part, or branch, has its own path for electric current. The electric current passes through each of them at the same time. If one branch of a parallel circuit is removed or broken, current will still flow through other branches. ▶

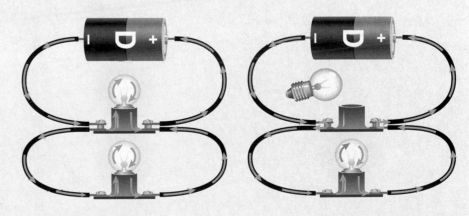

Magnetic Earth

Earth's magnetic field keeps humans and animals from getting lost.

The Earth is surrounded by a magnetic field. Why? Scientists don't know for sure, but most think it starts deep inside Earth, in its core. There, hot, liquid iron is constantly moving because of forces inside the core combined with Earth's rotation. Scientists believe this movement of hot metal is what gives Earth its magnetic field. It is as if there is a giant bar magnet inside Earth.

On the surface of the Earth, the magnetic field is not very strong, but it is very important. It is what makes compasses work. Inside each compass is a magnetized needle. One end of the needle is pointed or painted red. This is the "north-seeking" end. The needle sits on a loose base, so it can turn easily. The north-seeking end is attracted to one end of Earth's magnetic field— the end that points north. So the compass points north, too. Knowing this made it possible for early explorers to find their way, travel to new lands, and make maps.

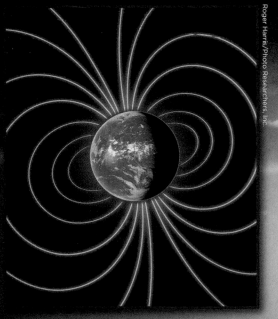

Roger Harris/Photo Researchers, Inc.

▲ The curved lines show Earth's magnetic field.

Harald Sund/Getty Images

Image Source

▲ The needle on a compass points north.

▲ Migrating birds use Earth's magnetic field to find their way.

When North Becomes South

If you could travel back in time 80 million years, and if you had a compass with you, you would probably get lost pretty quickly. The north-seeking needle on your compass would point south. That's because at that time—and many times before and since—Earth's magnetic field was reversed. It turns out that Earth's magnetic field can and does change.

Every so often—every 250,000 years, on average—Earth's magnetic field reverses completely. It has happened many, many times in Earth's history, and is likely to happen again. The reversal doesn't happen suddenly. It's a process than can take hundreds of thousands of years. Even so, big changes in Earth's magnetic field could make it tougher for humans and animals to find their way home. —*Lisa Jo Rudy*

Solar Interference

Heat and light from the Sun make life possible on Earth. But the Sun can sometimes cause problems for us too.

Our nearest star is a fiery ball of gas with a stormy surface that burns at 11,000 degrees Fahrenheit. Solar flares are bursts of energy that shoot far into space from the Sun's surface. Sunspots are cooler patches on the surface that form where the Sun's magnetic field is very strong.

Every 11 years the number of solar flares and sunspots increases. These bursts of energy can affect Earth's magnetic field and disrupt our communications systems. If we have astronauts in orbit, they can be harmed by the radiation.

SOHO-EIT Consortium/ESA/NASA

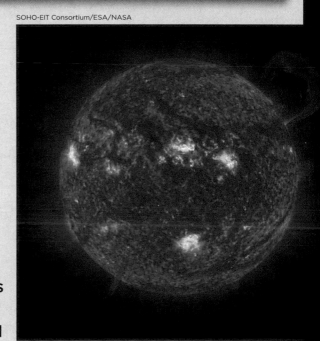

Solar flares and sunspots can cause problems on Earth.

Cause/Effect Writing Frame

Use the Writing Frame below to orally summarize "Circuits."

To make an electric current, you need a path **so** _____

_____ .

In a series circuit, the parts are _____

_____ .

As a result the current moves _____

_____ .

If any part of the series circuit is removed or broken, the circuit is open,

then _____

_____ .

In a parallel circuit each path, or branch, _____

_____ .

Therefore, if any branch of a parallel circuit is removed or breaks, _____

_____ .

Use the frame to write the summary on another sheet of paper.
Be sure to include the **bold** signal words. Keep this as a model of
this Text Structure.

Critical Thinking

1 A complete, unbroken circuit is called a _____.

    A. open circuit

    B. series circuit

    C. closed circuit

2 Find the paragraph in "Magnetic Earth" that explains how a compass works.

3 Find the sentence in "Magnetic Earth" that explains how often Earth's magnetic field reverses.

4 What do the diagrams on page 7 in "Circuits" tell you? Discuss this with a partner.

Diagrams are graphic aids that show how things relate to one another.

Digital Learning

For a list of links and activities that relate to this Science standard, visit the California Treasures Website at www.macmillanmh.com to access the Content Reader resources.

Have children view the e-Review "Electric Circuits."

EL In addition, distribute copies of the Translated Concept Summaries in Spanish, Chinese, Hmong, Khmer, and Vietnamese.

Electromagnets

In the 1820s and 1830s, scientists made some amazing discoveries about electric currents and magnets. They found that electric currents make magnetic fields and that magnets could make an electric current.

When an electric current flows through a wire, it creates a magnetic field around the wire. Increasing the current makes the magnetic field stronger. You can also make the magnetic field stronger by winding the wire into a long coil. Each loop of wire is like a little magnet that has its own magnetic force. The loops all push and pull in the same direction.

Electromagnets can make even stronger magnetic fields. An **electromagnet** is a coil of wire wrapped around a metal core, such as an iron bar. When an electric current flows through the coil, it creates a magnetic field. This magnetic field causes particles inside the metal core to line up. The metal core becomes magnetic. When the current stops, the metal core is no longer magnetic.

Electromagnets are often more useful than permanent magnets. Unlike a permanent magnet, an electromagnet can be switched on and off by turning the electric current on and off. Also, by changing the current, the magnetic field can be made stronger or weaker.

▲ Electric current in the wires turns this curved metal bar into a magnet.

Electromagnets are found in hundreds of devices, including electric guitars and power plant generators (JEN•uh•ray•tuhrz). They are used in the electric motors that power some trains and toy cars. They are used in transformers that increase or decrease the voltage of electric currents. They are found in many common appliances, such as vacuum cleaners and dishwashers.

Electromagnets are important parts of the loudspeakers in radios, televisions, and headphones. A **loudspeaker** is a device that changes electrical energy into sound. Sounds are produced when objects vibrate, or move back and forth quickly.

A device, such as a stereo, sends electric current to an electromagnet in the loudspeaker. The electromagnet is attached to a diaphragm (DIGH•uh•fram).

▲ Headphones are small loudspeakers with tiny electromagnets.

The diaphragm is the part of the loudspeaker that vibrates to create sound. The loudspeaker also has a permanent magnet. When electric current flows, the electromagnet is pushed and pulled by the permanent magnet. As the electromagnet moves, so does the diaphragm. The motion of the diaphragm produces sound.

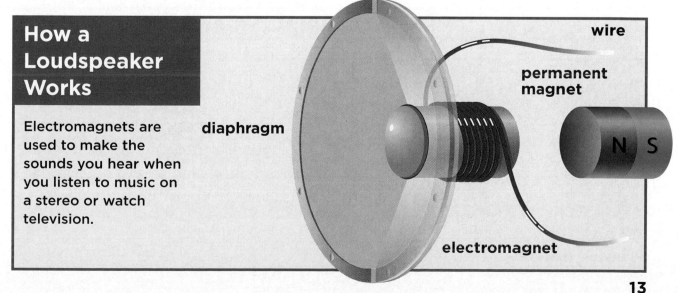

How a Loudspeaker Works

Electromagnets are used to make the sounds you hear when you listen to music on a stereo or watch television.

diaphragm

wire

permanent magnet

N S

electromagnet

ELECTRIFYING INVENTORS

Here's a look at some scientists who helped light up our world.

Everyone knows the name Thomas Edison. He and the people who worked with him invented the light bulb, the phonograph (record player), and many other electrical devices. But Edison had lots of "electrifying" company when it came to inventors.

Bettmann/Corbis

William Gilbert (1544–1603)
As early as the 1500s, Englishman William Gilbert was experimenting with electricity. Before Gilbert's work, people didn't even have a name for electricity! Gilbert conducted many experiments. He invented the terms *electricity*, *magnetic pole*, and *electric attraction*. Gilbert was the first person to figure out how the magnetic compass works.

The Granger Collection

Benjamin Franklin (1706–1790)
During the 1750s and 60s, the famous American Benjamin Franklin experimented with electricity. He discovered that lightning is really electricity and figured out how to generate static electricity. Franklin's inventions led the way to later inventions that changed the world.

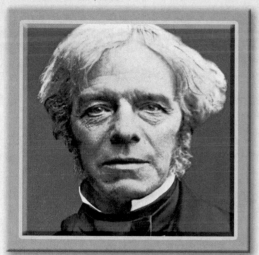

Hulton-Deutsch Collection/Corbis

Michael Faraday (1791–1867)

Michael Faraday was a scientist and inventor. He heard that another scientist had used electricity to make a magnet. Faraday was inspired. A few months later, he had invented the electric motor. Soon Faraday had figured out how to make an electric current. This discovery paved the way to electricity in our homes.

Courtesy Queens Borough Library

Lewis Latimer (1848–1928)

By the 1870s, Thomas Edison was busy trying to invent a usable electric light bulb. Businessman Hiram Maxim was trying to do the same. Maxim met Lewis Latimer, an expert draftsman. Latimer was also an inventor. Maxim told Latimer what he was trying to do. Latimer solved the problem. Thanks to Latimer's invention of a long-lasting light bulb, electricity could be used to light homes and streets.

Bettmann/Corbis

Grace Hopper (1906–1992)

In the 1940s, the first electronic computer was invented. In 1952, Grace Hopper, a computer scientist, invented the first computer "compiler." This software helped people "talk" to computers. Hopper created a special language called Common Business-Oriented Language. "COBOL" became the most popular business computing language in the world.

Compare/Contrast Writing Frame

Use the Writing Frame below to orally summarize "Electromagnets."

An electromagnet is _____

_____.

Both electromagnets and magnets _____

_____.

Unlike ordinary permanent magnets, electromagnets _____

_____.

Also, by changing the current, _____

_____.

Electromagnets can be found _____

_____.

Use the frame to write the summary on another sheet of paper.
Be sure to include the **bold** signal words. Keep this as a model of
this Text Structure.

Critical Thinking

1 If an electromagnet receives more current, it _____.

    A. becomes weaker

    B. becomes stronger

    C. turns off

2 Find the paragraph in "Electrifying Inventors" that tells about the light bulb. Who invented a long-lasting bulb?

3 Find the section in "Electrifying Inventors" that tells about Grace Hopper.

4 What does the diagram "How a Loudspeaker Works" on page 13 tell you? Discuss this with a partner.

Diagrams are graphic aids that show how things relate to one another.

Digital Learning

For a list of links and activities that relate to this Science standard, visit the California Treasures Web site at www.macmillanmh.com to access the Content Reader resources.

Have children view the e-Review "Electromagnets."

EL In addition, distribute copies of the Translated Concept Summaries in Spanish, Chinese, Hmong, Khmer, and Vietnamese.

Electricity

Just what is electricity? That's not so easy to answer. There are different kinds of electricity, but all electricity is the result of electrical charges. To understand electrical charge, you have to start with matter. Everything around you is made of matter. This book is made of matter. You are made of matter. Like color and hardness, **electrical charge** is a property of matter.

There are two types of electrical charges. These charges are called positive and negative. You cannot see or feel electrical charge the way you can see color or feel hardness. However, you can observe how charges interact with each other. A positive charge and a negative charge attract, or pull toward, each other. Positive charges repel, or push away, each other. Negative charges repel each other too.

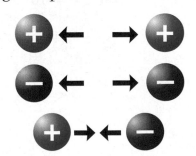

▲ Two positive (+) charges repel each other. So do negative (–) charges. Opposite charges attract each other.

▲ Charged particles in the girl's hair are attracted to the charged balloon.

People depend on electrical energy to light rooms, to cook food, and to power computers and air conditioners. Electric currents, or the flow of electrical charges, carry the energy that people use. Electrical devices change this energy into other kinds of energy, such as heat, light, and motion.

Electrical energy can be converted into heat. This heat can be used to cook food and dry clothes. Some furnaces use electrical energy to heat homes. Inside a hair dryer, electric current passes through wires which have a lot of resistance. This causes the wire to heat air inside the hair dryer.

Electrical energy is used to light buildings, vehicles, and streets. An incandescent (in•kuhn•DES•uhnt) bulb produces heat and light. Inside an incandescent bulb is a thin wire called a *filament*. As the filament resists electric current, it heats up and glows. A florescent (flaw•RES•uhnt) bulb uses a gas to produce light. Electric current makes the gas glow. Fluorescent bulbs do not become as hot as incandescent bulbs.

Electric motors change electrical energy into motion. Electric motors are found in toys, washing machines, drills, and other tools. Electric motors are also used to run trains at speeds as high as 515 kilometers (320 miles) per hour.

Electric energy is useful. However, it can also be dangerous. A short circuit might happen when the insulation on a wire frays. The bare wire touches a conductor, such as metal or another wire.

Since this connection has little resistance, it draws a large amount of electric current. This short circuit can heat up the wire and cause a fire.

Plugging too many devices into one outlet can also cause too much current to go through a wire. If this happens, the wire can overheat and may start a fire. To prevent this, most homes have many outlets that are connected to different circuits. No circuit carries too much current.

Circuit breakers and fuses also protect against dangerous amounts of electric current. A **circuit breaker** stops the flow of charges by switching off the current if it gets too high. A **fuse** breaks if the electric current in the circuit gets too high. This causes an open circuit.

Electrical energy inside the hair dryer is changed into heat energy. ▶

◄ When a circuit breaker breaks a circuit, it can be reset and used again.

When the Lights Go Out

Blackouts remind us how electricity runs our lives.

What happens when the lights go out? Power outages, also called blackouts, hit big cities the hardest. Traffic lights don't work, causing accidents and traffic jams. Subways and elevators stop, trapping thousands of people inside. Businesses lose money and time.

▲ A blackout, like this one in California, means no traffic lights and plenty of traffic jams.

Lights Out in California

In January, 2001, the lights went out in northern California. In many towns, traffic lights, bank machines, businesses, and classrooms all lost power. First one part of town went black. About an hour later, the lights went on, and another part of town lost its electricity. Each area lost power for only an hour or two—but in that time there were all kinds of problems. There were traffic accidents. Businesses stopped working. Some schools shut down.

These power outages were called "rotating blackouts." They were planned by the Pacific Gas and Electric Company. California had not built any new power plants for years. The demand for electricity was huge, but no one had figured out where to get the power or how to pay for it. Finally, the lights went out.

During a 2003 blackout, thousands of New Yorkers walk home over the Brooklyn Bridge. ▼

The Great Blackout of 1965

November 9, 1965, was a chilly day. As usual, people throughout the northeastern part of the United States and Canada were using lots of power to heat and light their homes and run businesses. At 5:15 P.M., an electrical relay in Toronto, Canada, failed. A surge of electricity caused the local power lines to shut down for safety. The electricity, however, had to go somewhere. Because the electrical lines from Canada were connected with those in the United States, the electricity traveled down the line.

Everywhere it went, it overloaded the system. The system shut down. At 5:18 P.M., the lights were off in Rochester, New York. Boston went dark at 5:21. New York City lost power at 5:28.

By 5:30, 80,000 square miles of the Northeast were in darkness. Almost 800,000 people were stuck in the New York subways. It took until midnight to free most of the passengers. By early the next morning, power had returned to New York and the entire Northeast. —Lisa Jo Rudy

AP Photo

Top Blackouts in the United States

April 15, 2003
50 million people are left in the dark in New York, NY; Albany, NY; Hartford, CT; Detroit, MI; Cleveland, OH; and Toronto, Ontario in Canada.

November 9, 1965
25 million people are affected by a blackout that hits Canada, New England, and New York.

July 13, 1977
9 million people in New York are without power.

January 28, 1965
2 million people in Iowa and portions of five other Midwestern states are affected by a blackout.

▲ People wait in line to use a pay phone during New York's 1965 blackout.

Description Writing Frame

Use the Writing Frame below to orally summarize "Electricity."

All electricity is the result of _____.

Electric currents, or the flow of electrical charges, _____

_____.

Electrical devices change this energy into other kinds of energy,

such as _____.

For example, heat can be used _____

_____.

Electric energy can also be used as light. **For example**, _____

_____.

Electric motors convert energy to motion and are found in things

such as _____

_____.

Electric energy can be very useful.

Use the frame to write the summary on another sheet of paper.
Be sure to include the **bold** signal words. Keep this as a model of
this Text Structure.

Critical Thinking

1 Electrical charges can be _____ .

    A. positive

    B. negative

    C. positive and negative

2 What is a rotating blackout? Find the paragraph in "When the Lights Go Out" that explains it.

3 Find the sentence in "Electricity" that explains how charges interact with each other.

4 Read the caption for the picture of California on page 20. Talk about this caption with a partner. What added information does it give that is not in the text?

Photographs and captions give the reader additional information about the subject of the article.

Digital Learning

For a list of links and activities that relate to this Science standard, visit the California Treasures Web site at www.macmillanmh.com to access the Content Reader resources.

Have children view the e-Review "Using Electrical Energy."

EL In addition, distribute copies of the Translated Concept Summaries in Spanish, Chinese, Hmong, Khmer, and Vietnamese.

Science

Macmillan/McGraw-Hill

Magnets

You may have played with magnets and watched them snap together or push apart. Magnets can also make some objects move or even fly through the air. A magnet can affect an object without even touching it.

When you bring two magnets close together, they will either repel or attract each other. The force that pushes magnets apart or pulls them together is called magnetic force. A **magnet** is any object with magnetic force.

The parts of a magnet where the magnetic force is strongest are called the magnetic **poles**. All known magnets have two poles— a north pole and a south pole. When two magnets are brought together, a north pole and a south pole attract each other. Like poles (north-north or south-south) repel each other.

Magnets that are far apart do not pull or push enough to move each other. The magnetic force between two magnets is weak when magnets are far apart. The magnetic force gets stronger as the magnets are brought closer together.

▼ Magnetic force pulls opposite poles together and pushes like poles apart.

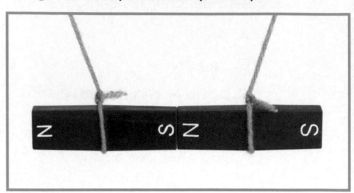

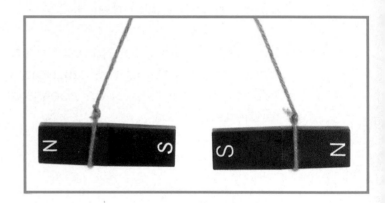

The aurora australis is a display of lights near the South Pole. Charged particles from the Sun become caught in Earth's magnetic field and give off light.

Every magnet has a magnetic field around it. A **magnetic field** is the area of magnetic force around a magnet. When one magnet enters the magnetic field of another magnet, it is either attracted or repelled. This can happen even if the magnets are not touching. A magnet's magnetic field is strongest near the magnet's poles. The magnetic field is weaker farther away from the poles.

Did you know our planet is actually a giant magnet? Much of the inside of Earth is made up of melted iron. This iron creates a magnetic field that surrounds our planet.

Earth spins around its axis, an imaginary line through the center of Earth. The geographic (jee•uh•GRAF•ik) North Pole is located at one end of this axis. The geographic South Pole is located at the other end.

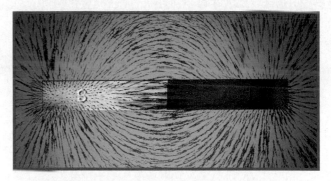

▲ Iron filings can be used to show the magnetic field of a bar magnet. Magnetic field lines curve from one pole to the other.

Earth has one magnetic pole near its geographic North Pole. There is another magnetic pole near the geographic South Pole.

Long ago, people noticed that one end of a magnet turned to point north. They called this end the north-seeking pole. The other end was named the south-seeking pole, because it pointed south. Today those names are shortened to just the north pole and the south pole of a magnet.

Welcome Aboard the Flying Trains!

A train that floats on air and has no wheels may sound like a dream of the future, but it's real, and it's here today.

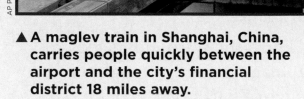
AP Photo

▲ **A maglev train in Shanghai, China, carries people quickly between the airport and the city's financial district 18 miles away.**

You're traveling at 310 miles per hour on a cushion of air. Your vehicle is streamlined and looks a lot like a rocket. It's not a rocket, though. It's a maglev (short for "magnetic levitation") train. Just like the name says, maglev trains have magnets that levitate (raise) the train just a little bit above the tracks. Because there's no friction and the trains are designed for speed, maglev trains can move incredibly fast.

Magnetic "Magic"

How do maglev trains work? They start with a large electromagnet. Electromagnets work like ordinary magnets, except that their magnetic power is created by an electric current. While the electric current is running through the wires, the magnet attracts and repels just like an ordinary magnet.

When the electric current is turned off, the magnet stops working too. Maglev trains have large electromagnets attached under each car.

Maglev trains run on special tracks. Along the tracks are electrified coils of wire. When the electricity is turned on, the coils of wire are magnetized. The magnets in the tracks repel (push away) the magnets in the trains. The power of the magnets pushing against each other makes the trains float about half an inch above the track.

Once the train is floating, it's time for the train to move. Electromagnets are also responsible for moving the train forward. The magnets in front of the train pull the train forward, while the magnets behind the train push. Because the train is floating, there are no wheels to push and no parts to wear out. Maglev trains can run very fast, create almost no pollution, and need little maintenance.

Maglev Trains of the Future

China and Japan were the first countries to put maglev trains into regular use. Other countries, including England, Germany, and the United States, are expected to have maglev train service in the near future. —*Lisa Jo Rudy*

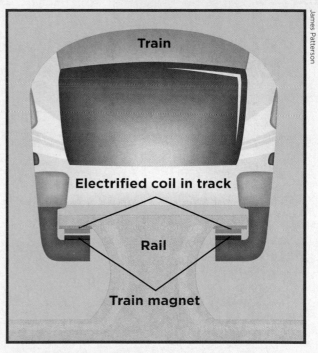

James Patterson

▲ **Electrified coils in the track repel magnets on the train, causing the maglev train to "levitate."**

Bernd Mellmann / Alamy

In Shanghai, China, a maglev train seems to fly over the highway below.

Sequence Writing Frame

**Use the Writing Frame below to orally summarize
"Welcome Aboard the Flying Trains!"**

Maglev is short for _____

_____ .

How do maglev trains work? They **start** with _____

_____ .

Next, trains run _____

_____ .

Then, the power of the magnets pushing against each other makes

_____

_____ .

Finally, _____

_____ .

Use the frame to write the summary on another sheet of paper.
Be sure to include the **bold** signal words. Keep this as a model of
this Text Structure.

Critical Thinking

1　A magnetic field is the area of _____ around a magnet.

　　A. magnetic force

　　B. magnetic poles

　　C. magnetic particles

2　Maglev trains can move incredibly fast. Reread the sentence in "Welcome Aboard the Flying Trains!" that explain why.

3　Point out the paragraph in "Magnets" that discusses how the north and south poles of magnets were named.

4　Find the picture on page 25 of the magnetic field of a bar magnet. Do you think the Earth's magnetic field looks the same or different? Discuss in a small group.

Photographs and captions give the reader additional information about the subject of the article.

Digital Learning

For a list of links and activities that relate to this Science standard, visit the California Treasures Website at www.macmillanmh.com to access the Content Reader resources.

Have children view the e-Review "Magnets."

EL In addition, distribute copies of the Translated Concept Summaries in Spanish, Chinese, Hmong, Khmer, and Vietnamese

Science
Macmillan/McGraw-Hill

Plants

Plants are living things. They do much more than just add beauty to our world. Plants give us the food we eat and some of the clothes we wear. They even give off a gas that we breathe, called oxygen (OK•shu•juhn). Without plants, Earth would be an empty place. With plants, our planet is bursting with life.

Although plants differ in their shapes and sizes, most plants are alike in one way. They make their own food in a process called **photosynthesis** (foh•toh•SIN•thuh•suhs). All organisms, or living things, need energy to grow, stay healthy, and reproduce. Reproduce means to make more of one's own kind. Plants get the energy they need from the food they make.

During photosynthesis, plants take in sunlight, water, and a gas in the air called carbon dioxide. Plants use these things to make sugar, which is a plant's source of food and energy.

Photosynthesis

Plants take in sunlight.

Plants give off oxygen.

Plants take in carbon dioxide.

Plants take in water and nutrients from the soil.

Animals depend on plants for food energy.

Most plants need photosynthesis to survive and grow. Did you know that you need photosynthesis too? In fact, most animals depend on plants making their own food. Why?

Animals cannot make their own food the way plants can. Instead they must eat other organisms to get the energy they need. Plants provide the energy that travels from one organism to another. Plants capture energy from the Sun to make their own food.

They use most of their food energy as they grow and reproduce. They also store some energy in their roots, stems, leaves, and other structures. When an animal, such as a grasshopper, eats a plant, stored energy passes from the plant to the animal. The animal uses most of this energy to grow and reproduce. It also stores some energy. When an animal, such as a bird, eats the grasshopper, stored energy passes to the bird. In this way, most animals depend on plants for energy.

31

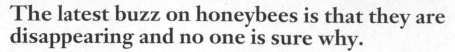

Bad News for Bees

The latest buzz on honeybees is that they are disappearing and no one is sure why.

Where have all the bees gone? Beekeepers, researchers, and farmers are buzzing. They want to know why millions of honeybees are disappearing. The bees are leaving no clues and no dead bodies behind. "The bees have vanished," says Jerry Bromenshenk, a bee expert.

Twenty-four states have spotted big problems with local bee colonies. A colony is a large group of bees that live and work together.

HHS/The Plain Dealer/Landov

▲ A beekeeper examines a hive.

It's possible that more states have lost bees. Honey production is way down across the nation.

Busy, Busy Bees

Honeybees are hardworking insects. Of course, they make honey. They also help flowering plants grow and thrive. Bees move grains of pollen from one part of a flower to another so a plant can grow seeds and fruit. This process, called pollination, is important for crops like apples, almonds, cucumbers, and cranberries. Crops, and the farmers who grow them, could be in trouble if there aren't enough bees to do the job.

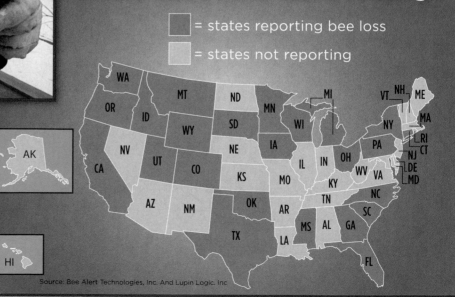

Where Bees Have Gone Missing

= states reporting bee loss

= states not reporting

Source: Bee Alert Technologies, Inc. And Lupin Logic, Inc

How Bees Work

Fruits and vegetables can't grow unless they're pollinated. Along with birds, bats, and other insects, honeybees are among nature's most important pollinators.

First, honeybees crawl around a plant blossom. While they collect nectar from the blossom, the bees' legs become coated with pollen. Then the bees fly to another blossom. There, some of the pollen from the first blossom lands on the second blossom. Now a fruit or vegetable can grow.

Bees don't always just happen to show up on farms where crops are grown. To make sure their crops are pollinated, farmers rent colonies of bees. Beekeepers let the bees out to pollinate the crops. Then the bees return to their boxes, and they are moved to the next farm. If honeybees don't pollinate, many crops won't produce fruit and seeds. Honeybees pollinate about one third of the crops in the world!

A "Bee-g" Problem to Solve

Experts met in Florida in February 2007 to work on solving the mystery of the missing bees. A disease could be killing the bees. Hot dry weather could be to blame. No one knows.

Groups connected to the bee biz are pooling money to try to stop the crisis. Everyone hopes to see the bees bounce back. —*Andrea Delbanco*

Joe Raedle/Getty Images

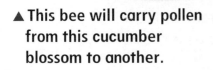

▲ This bee will carry pollen from this cucumber blossom to another.

Jack Fields/Corbis

Bees from these rented hives will help ensure a good crop.

Problem/Solution Writing Frame

Use the Writing Frame below to orally summarize "Bad News for Bees."

Millions of honeybees are disappearing.

As a result, _____

_____

_____ .

Honeybees also help with _____

_____

_____ .

If honeybees don't _____ , **then** _____

_____

_____ .

To solve this _____

_____ .

Everyone hopes to see the bees bounce back.

Use the frame to write the summary on another sheet of paper. Be sure to include the **bold** signal words. Keep this as a model of this Text Structure.

Critical Thinking

1 During photosynthesis a plant uses all of the following except
_____ .

    A. sugar

    B. sunlight

    C. carbon dioxide

2 Locate the paragraph in "Bad News for Bees" that explains how honeybees pollinate.

3 Find the sentences in "Plants" that explain the importance of plants.

4 Talk about the map on page 32 with a partner. What does the map tell you?

Maps are drawings of geographic locations such as a city, state, or park.

Digital Learning

For a list of links and activities that relate to this Science standard, visit the California Treasures Website at www.macmillanmh.com to access the Content Reader resources.

Have children view the e-Review "Plants and Sunlight."

EL In addition, distribute copies of the Translated Concept Summaries in Spanish, Chinese, Hmong, Khmer, and Vietnamese.

The Food Chain

Living things need energy to live and grow. They get energy from food. A **food chain** shows how energy passes from one organism to another as food. First a plant uses the Sun's energy to make its own food. Next an animal, such as an insect, eats the plant. Then another animal, such as a bird, eats that insect. Energy passes from the Sun to the plant to the insect to the bird.

Green plants in a food chain are called **producers**. They are called this because they make, or produce, their own food. Animals are called **consumers**. Animals cannot make their own food. They must eat, or consume, plants or other animals for food.

Mountain Food Chain

A mustard plant takes in energy from the Sun to make its own food. ▼

Solar energy is the main source of energy for life on Earth.

Herbivores are animals that eat mainly plants. They are known as **primary consumers** because they are the first consumer in a food chain. Animals that eat other animals are called **carnivores**. Some animals seem to eat everything. Animals that eat both plants and animals are called **omnivores**.

Most food chains are similar in a few ways. Sunlight is at the beginning of nearly all food chains. A plant, or producer, is next in the chain. Then an animal eats the plant. Next another animal eats the plant eater. The chain continues until tiny living things break down organisms and return nutrients to the soil. These tiny living things are decomposers. The nutrients they return to the soil are used by new plants, and the chain begins again.

With each step of the food chain, matter and energy pass from one organism to another. Because organisms use most of the energy in food to live and grow, only a small amount of energy is passed from organism to organism.

▲ A gopher eats the mustard plant.

A weasel eats the gopher. ▶

A mountain lion eats the weasel. ▶

▲ When the mountain lion dies, its body is broken down by decomposers.

Welcome Back, Grizzly Bears

Grizzly bears in Yellowstone National Park are off the endangered species list, but they still need protection.

franzfoto.com / Alamy

▲ **A female grizzly and her cub in Yellowstone National Park.**

Grizzly bears in Yellowstone National Park, in Wyoming, have been removed from the endangered species list. The bears were given threatened status in 1975, when their population numbered 300 or fewer. Now there are more than 500 grizzlies in Yellowstone, thanks to hard work and caring people.

Grizzly bears, also called brown bears, stand about 7 feet tall and weigh up to 600 pounds. These meat-eaters are at the top of the food chain and face little threat from other wild animals. But humans, who sometimes kill the bears out of fear for their own safety, hunt grizzlies. Humans also build homes and businesses near grizzly habitat. This is hard on the bears, which need a lot of room to roam.

WYOMING

MONTANA

Yellowstone National Park

IDAHO

WYOMING

UTAH

COLORADO

Time for Kids

Bringing Bears Back

"The key to the success story is preventing bears from dying," says Chris Servheen of the U.S. Fish and Wildlife Service. Officials closed roads to protect the bears' habitat and took steps to help bears and visitors live together in the park. "Because fewer bears die, more bears live to have cubs," Servheen told TFK.

But not all grizzlies are out of the woods. Four other grizzly populations in the lower 48 states remain listed as threatened.

Some people think that the Yellowstone bears were taken off the list too soon. A group of more than 250 scientists and researchers sent a letter to the government protesting the delisting. Servheen is confident that the grizzlies will be okay. "We have detailed monitoring systems in place," he says. "If there are any problems, we can respond. —*Andrea Delbanco*

AP Photo

▲ **All grizzlies in the lower 48 states need protection.**

Erwin and Peggy Bauer/Animals Animals

Why Grizzlies Matter

Anything that benefits the grizzly bear probably benefits many other animals.

Grizzly bears often share their habitat with black bears, wolves, deer, and elk. Grizzlies eat cutthroat trout, white bark pine nuts, and other animals and plants. A healthy grizzly population usually means the populations of other animals and plants in its habitat will do well too.

Compare/Contrast Writing Frame

Use the Writing Frame below to orally summarize "The Food Chain."

All living things need energy to live and grow.

Green plants are called _____.

Animals are called _____.

Both producers and consumers get energy from _____.

In some ways, however, _____

and _____ are **different**.

They are **different** because producers _____

_____.

Consumers are **different** from producers because _____

_____.

So _____ and _____
are **alike** in some ways and **different** in others.

Use the frame to write the summary on another sheet of paper. Be sure to include the **bold** signal words. Keep this as a model of this Text Structure.

Critical Thinking

1 Which type of organism makes its own food?

    A. producer

    B. decomposer

    C. consumer

2 Find the sentence in "Welcome Back, Grizzly Bears" that tells where grizzlies fit into the food chain.

3 Find the section in "The Food Chain" that discusses the difference between herbivores, carnivores, and omnivores.

4 What does the inset map on page 38 show you?

An inset map is an enlargement of a small section of the map.

Digital Learning

For a list of links and activities that relate to this Science standard, visit the California Treasures Web site at www.macmillanmh.com to access the Content Readers resources.

Have children view the e-Review "Food Chains."

EL In addition, distribute copies of the Translated Concept Summaries in Spanish, Chinese, Hmong, Khmer, and Vietnamese.

Decomposers

Each fall and winter, thousands of leaves fall to the forest floor. Some trees also fall down. Some of this plant material is gone by the following spring. There are fewer dead leaves on the ground. The fallen trees are rotting away.

Who or what is responsible for this cleanup? Decomposers do this important job for an environment. **Decomposers** break down organisms that are no longer living. They break them down into nutrients that can be used again by plants.

▲ The decomposers growing on this fallen log are called fungi. They slowly break down the log.

▲ Most earthworms eat plant life that has already died. Earthworms pass nutrients from dead plants to the soil.

There are many types of decomposers. Each breaks down a special type of organism. For example, earthworms break down only plants. Plantlike organism called **fungi** (FUN•jigh) break down rotting wood and other plant parts. Still other decomposers break down what is left of dead animals. Decomposers that consume dead matter are also consumers.

Decomposers work together to break down organisms completely. The once-living material may become part of the soil. This material adds nutrients to soil that help plants to grow well. Now the food chain can start all over again.

Some insects, such as this beetle, are decomposers. Other insect decomposers include flies and wasps. ▶

43

Food to Flowers

A California program is showing kids how to recycle school lunch leftovers into food for plants.

You know that eating a healthy lunch is good for you. Now your lunch leftovers can be a healthy food source for plants! A program in San Francisco, California, called *Food to Flowers!* is turning leftover school lunches into compost—a natural fertilizer for plants. California has lots of other ideas on how to reduce, reuse, and recycle almost everything.

What Is Compost?

Compost is made in a natural process that breaks down organic matter. Organic matter is anything that was once living. Leaves, grass, paper (which comes from trees), and most types of food can be turned into compost. The organic material is mixed together. Small living things called decomposers start to break it down almost immediately. Insects, earthworms and other worms, and fungi are all decomposers. They live in the organic material. Over time, decomposers turn organic matter into a dark, crumbly material that looks like soil. It is full of good things that help plants grow.

Phoebe the Phoenix, the *Food to Flowers!* mascot ▶

Les Gibbon/Alamy

Courtesy SF Environment

How *Food to Flowers!* Works

Food to Flowers! places big green carts in school lunchrooms. After lunch, kids toss in all their leftover food scraps and soiled paper products. A local waste hauler takes the carts filled with lunch scraps to a nearby composting facility. There leftovers are ground up into very small pieces and turned into compost. Some of the compost is sold to local organic farms. Some is also given back to the schools to use in their gardens.

Composting turns leftover food and paper products into something useful that is also good for the environment. The same leftovers would otherwise be hauled off to big landfills as trash.

Other Great Ideas for the Environment

Food to Flowers! may not be available in your school. But another program, called Waste-Free Lunch, was created for every kid in every school. When you pack a waste-free lunch, you cut down on plastics and other non-recyclable materials that are tossed into the trash. —*Lisa Jo Rudy*

Courtesy SF Environment

▲ **Kids dump their lunch leftovers into a *Food to Flowers!* cart.**

Here's How to Pack a Waste-Free Lunch

Do Include

- Sandwiches in reusable containers
- Whole fruits without packaging
- Drinks in containers that can be reused, such as thermoses, or recycled, such as cans
- Snacks bought in bulk and brought in reusable containers
- Reusable cloth napkin
- Reusable utensils

Don't Include

- Individually wrapped snacks
- Plastic bags that are not reusable
- Disposable forks and spoons

Sequence Writing Frame

Use the Writing Frame below to orally summarize "Food to Flowers."

A California program called *Food to Flowers!* is turning leftover

school lunches into compost. Compost is made from _____

_____.

First, *Food to Flowers!* _____

_____.

After lunch _____

_____.

Next _____

_____.

Then the leftovers _____

_____.

Finally some of the compost _____

_____.

Use the frame to write the summary on another sheet of paper.
Be sure to include the **bold** signal words. Keep this as a model of
this Text Structure.

Critical Thinking

1 Fungi break down _____.

    A. plants

    B. animals

    C. wood and plant parts

2 Find the sentence in "Food to Flowers" that describes organic matter.

3 Point to the word on page 42 that defines what is responsible for the breakdown of organisms that are no longer living.

4 Orally create your own caption for the photo on page 45.

Photographs and captions give visual examples that help explain what the text states.

Digital Learning

For a list of links and activities that relate to this Science standard, visit the California Treasures Web site at www.macmillanmh.com to access the Content Readers resources.

Have children view the Science in Motion "Microorganisms at Work."

EL In addition, distribute copies of the Translated Concept Summaries in Spanish, Chinese, Hmong, Khmer, and Vietnamese.

Ecosystems

Plants make their home in soil. Birds may use grasses to make nests. Bacteria in the soil break down leaves. Living and nonliving things interact, or have an effect on one another, every day. An **ecosystem** (EE•koh•sys•tuhm) is all the interacting parts of an environment. An ecosystem can be large, such as a redwood forest, or small, such as a pond.

Large or small, ecosystems are made up of living and nonliving things. The living things that shape an ecosystem are called **biotic factors** (bigh•AH•tik•FAK•tuhrz).

The nonliving things that shape an ecosystem are called **abiotic factors** (ay•bigh•AH•tik•FAK•tuhrz). Temperature, rainfall, snow, ice, sunlight, and soil are abiotic factors.

Ponds, deserts, rain forests and coral reefs are just a few examples of ecosystems. Each has a different climate, soil, and organisms.

Pond Ecosystem

❶ Many plants find space to live along the water's edge. They get water and nutrients from the soil.

❷ Birds use pond plants to make their nests.

❸ Frogs feast on the insects they find around the pond.

❹ Turtles come to the water's surface to get air and warmth from the Sun.

Think of the abiotic factors in a pond ecosystem. You might think of water and soil. Now add the biotic factors in and around the pond. Both of these factors together make up the ecosystem.

The biotic and abiotic factors of an ecosystem work together. For example, plants in a pond need a lot of water. They also need a certain kind of soil to grow well. Pond animals need a special climate (KLIGH•muht). Climate describes the typical weather patterns of an area over time.

Stop the Spartina!

A group of Washington elementary-school kids take on an alien invader—a weed!

Poor spartina! It's a perfectly good plant when it stays where it belongs. But it doesn't belong in Washington State's Puget Sound. There it has turned into a fast-spreading, life-choking weed.

Plants and animals that wind up in the wrong place are called aliens or exotics by ecologists. Spartina, or cordgrass, is native to many East Coast waterways, but in Washington, it is an alien species.

Jack Thomas

▲ **The Lincoln Elementary students who took on the spartina problem**

An Alien Attacks

Spartina spreads easily. In many parts of Puget Sound, it has crowded out native plants. Even worse, spartina grows in thick clumps. The clumps change the mudflats around the Sound. This affects the entire ecosystem. As native plants and the gentle slopes of the mudflats disappear, native animals like crabs, snails, salmon, and shorebirds have less to eat. That makes them leave the area.

The kids at Lincoln Elementary School in Mount Vernon, Washington, decided to take on the spartina problem. At first they didn't know anything about the plant. Their research told them an interesting story.

Galen Rowell/Mountain Light/Alamy

▲ **Spartina grows in thick clumps that harm the mudflats.**

Where Did It Come From?

The trouble started in the late 1800s. Settlers from the East came to the West to raise oysters. They brought the oysters packed in wet spartina to keep them fresh. When the oysters were put in Puget Sound, spartina seeds that had come along for the ride sprouted.

Spartina was also introduced to the area on purpose. Duck hunters planted it hoping to attract more ducks. Engineers used it to control erosion. Farmers planted it to feed their cattle.

▼ **Spartina threatens beautiful Puget Sound.**

Taking Action

Getting rid of spartina won't be easy. It will take a lot of hard work, money, and time. That's why the Lincoln Elementary students felt their most important job was educating parents, politicians, and the public. They held town meetings and traveled to the state capitol in Olympia to talk about the spartina problem. They went to a bay in Puget Sound to snip off spartina seed heads to keep the weed from spreading.

It took decades for the spartina problem to take root; it will take many years to fix it. —*David Bjerklie*

Terry Donnelly

Description Writing Frame

Use the Writing Frame below to orally summarize "Ecosystems."

Ecosystems have many interesting **characteristics**. An ecosystem is

_____

_____

_____ .

One characteristic of an ecosystem is the _____

_____ .

Biotic factors _____

_____ .

Another interesting characteristic is _____

_____

or aboiotic factors.

Because of these characteristics, an ecosystem can be large
or small.

Use the frame to write the summary on another sheet of paper.
Be sure to include the **bold** signal words. Keep this as a model of
this Text Structure.

Critical Thinking

1 Plants, animals and microorganisms are _____ .

    A. abiotic factors

    B. biotic factors

    C. critical factors

2 Find the sentence in "Stop the Spartina!" that explains what aliens or exotics are.

3 Point to the place in the text "Ecosystems" that mentions the role of climate on an ecosystem.

4 Look at the diagram on page 48. How do the living and nonliving things in the pond interact?

Captions help explain the diagram.

Digital Learning

For a list of links and activities that relate to this Science standard, visit the California Treasures Web site at www.macmillanmh.com to access the Content Readers resources.

Have children view the e-Review "Ecosystems."

EL In addition, distribute copies of the Translated Concept Summaries in Spanish, Chinese, Hmong, Khmer, and Vietnamese.

Changing Ecosystems

It may be hard to notice, but ecosystems are always changing. Over time ecosystems can become warmer or colder, wetter or drier. Over millions of years the land itself can change. Mountain ranges can be built up and broken down. Lakes can dry up or fill in. Some changes affect living things and make it difficult for them to survive.

Some living things can survive changes by changing their behaviors and habits. An **accommodation** (uh•kom•uh•DAY•shuhn) is an individual organism's response to change. For example, the main food supply of some animals may be wiped out by a fire. To survive, some animals will change what they eat. They may also survive with less food by being less active. Some animals will use new plants or materials as shelter.

Not all animals can accommodate ecosystem changes. Food and clean water may be hard to find after a fire. Some animals must find a new place to live. There they will look for food, water, and shelter.

Some changes can be good for an ecosystem. A fire can keep an ecosystem from becoming too crowded. Overcrowding can keep plants and animals from meeting their needs.

▼ A fire can change a forest ecosystem quickly. Some organisms can survive through ecosystem changes.

Some living things that do not move after an ecosystem change can slowly die out. An animal or plant that has very few left of its kind is **endangered** (en•DAYN•juhrd). Some endangered plants and animals become **extinct** (ek•STINGKT). This means there are none left of their kind.

When an ecosystem changes, many animals use adaptations to survive. **Adaptations** are special features or behaviors that help living things survive in their environment. A fish's gills, a dragonfly's wings, and an eagle's sharp eyesight are adaptations. Adaptations can help animals move, catch food, and live in certain climates.

Adaptations can also help living things protect themselves. For example, some animals hide by blending into their environment.

This adaptation is called **camouflage** (KA•muh•flahzh). Some animals hide by looking like other organisms. This adaptation is called **mimicry** (MI•mi•kree).

Can one plant or animal adapt for survival on its own? No. Think of a giraffe's long neck. This trait was passed down from one generation to the next. Long ago many giraffes' necks were much shorter. The tallest giraffes that reached leaves in trees could get more food. These giraffes survived. Over time giraffes with shorter necks died out. The study of how organisms pass traits from one generation to the next is called **genetics** (juh•NET•iks).

▲ Can you find the Indian leaf butterfly in this picture? Mimicry helps it hide in plain sight.

▲ A giraffe's long neck helps it to reach leaves and see predators.

55

A Very Hairy Crab

Scientists discover a new species of crab off the coast of Easter Island.

Crabs come in lots of different colors—red, blue, brown, and green. Now, however, scientists have discovered a new species of crab—one that is covered in blonde "fur."

In 2006, scientists announced they had found the weird crab. It was caught by a joint U.S.-French team in water 7,540 feet deep near Easter Island in the Pacific Ocean.

The creature's scientific name is *Kiwa hirsuta. Kiwa* comes from the name of the Polynesian goddess of shellfish. *Hirsuta* means "hairy." Scientists also nicknamed it the Yeti.

"This is a very rare find," said Joe Jones, one of the scientists. He said it shows, "how little we know about the ocean."

A Family of Its Own

Kiwa hirsuta is not just a new species of crustacean. Scientists say it belongs in a new family all its own. It is about six inches long. Its body has no color. The fur, or hair, covers its pincers. Some other crab species have similar hair.

▼ *Kiwa hirsuta,* nicknamed the Yeti, from above and below

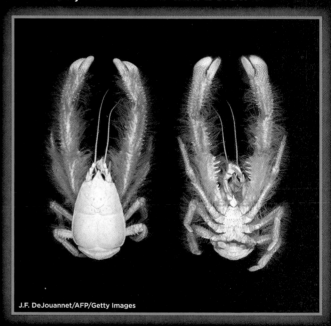

J.F. DeJouannet/AFP/Getty Images

▼ The new crab was found among other deep-water crustaceans.

Ralph White/Corbis

MBari/B. Vrijenhoek/Newscom

▲ The filaments on the Yeti's legs contain lots of bacteria.

Scientist Michel Segonzac works for the French Research Institute for Exploitation of the Sea. He is one of the researchers who discovered the crab. He says that the filaments around the pincers contain lots of bacteria. It's possible the bacteria filter out harmful poisons in the water. They help the crab to survive.

Like many deep-sea animals, *Kiwa hirsuta* is blind. Since there is almost no light at that depth of the ocean, animals there have no need for sight.

Deep Ocean Vents

The hairy crab lives in a strange world of deep ocean vents. Most of the deep ocean floor is almost lifeless. Light cannot get past the first 300 feet of seawater. Below that depth most algae cannot live. Without algae, there is no food chain of fish and other animals.

But in some places there are vents that release gasses and hot water. The water is heated by volcanic activity. These are called hydrothermal vents. The heat is a source of energy, and some strange sea creatures have adapted to use it.

Giant tubeworms and huge clams live near deep-sea vents in the Pacific Ocean. In the Atlantic Ocean, the vents are home to eyeless shrimp. The hairy crab now joins the list of odd animals that survive in this very special environment. —*Richie Chevat*

Ralph White/Corbis

▲ Giant tubeworms like these live near hydrothermal vents.

Cause/Effect Writing Frame

**Use the Writing Frame below to orally summarize
"A Very Hairy Crab."**

The Kiwa hirsuta lives deep in the Pacific Ocean. There is

almost no light that deep in the ocean, **as a result** _____

_____ .

Kiwa hirsuta is about _____

long, and its body has _____

_____ .

The _____

_____

contain bacteria. **Because of this** _____

_____ .

Hydrothermal vents are a source of energy deep in the ocean.

This explains why _____

_____ .

Use the frame to write the summary on another sheet of paper.
Be sure to include the **bold** signal words. Keep this as a model
of this Text Structure.

Critical Thinking

1 In individual organism's response to a change in the ecosystem is called _____ .

    A. accommodation

    B. adaptation

    C. genetics

2 Locate text in "A Very Hairy Crab" that explains what *Kiwa hirsuta* means.

3 Point to the definition of mimicry in "Changing Ecosystems."

4 Look at the picture on the bottom of page 54. With a partner describe another picture you could use to show how an ecosystem can change.

Photographs provide visual examples of facts or ideas that appear in a text.

Digital Learning

For a list of links and activities that relate to this Science standard, visit the California Treasures Web site at www.macmillanmh.com to access the Content Readers resources.

Have children view the e-Review "Changes in Ecosystems."

EL In addition, distribute copies of the Translated Concept Summaries in Spanish, Chinese, Hmong, Khmer, and Vietnamese.

Pollination and Seed Dispersal

Flowers depend on animals in many ways. Flowering plants reproduce when male cells are transported to female cells. This process is called **pollination** (pah·luh·NAY·shuhn).

Animals such as bees, hummingbirds, wasps, butterflies and bats help with pollination. They travel from flower to flower and collect a sweet drink inside the flower called **nectar** (NEK·tuhr). As an animal visits a flower, a powdery material called **pollen** (PAH·luhn) rubs off the flower and onto the animal's body.

When the animal visits another flower, some of this pollen rubs off on the flower. The animal does not know this, but the powder helps the flower reproduce.

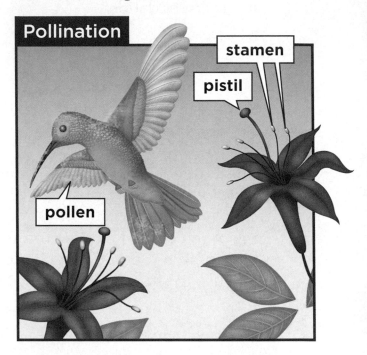

Pollination

stamen

pistil

pollen

When a bee lands on a flower, pollen collects on its body.

▲ This iguana is eating a punta cactus fruit. The seeds inside the fruit are dispersed in the animal's waste.

How do the seeds inside fruit get planted in the ground? **Seed dispersal** (SEED•di•SPUHR•suhl) is the process of spreading seeds. During this process, seeds are left in a place where they can grow into new plants. Animals play an important part in dispersing, or spreading, seeds.

An animal eats a fruit and its seeds. The seeds are later left on the ground in the animal's waste. The seeds may grow into a new plant.

Some plants have sticky seeds. These seeds can easily stick to an animal's fur. When the animal moves to a new place, the seeds rub off. They fall to the ground. Here they may grow into new plants.

Merlin D. Tuttle, Bat Conservation International

Bats About Bats

You may think bats have a bad reputation, but they do a lot of good.

What do you think of when you think of bats? Vampires? Scary movies? What could be creepier than a world full of bats? A world without bats!

Bats have done little to earn their bad reputation. Most bats, including California's brown bat and the Mexican long-tongued bat, are harmless. Instead of drinking human blood, they eat insects and fruit. More importantly, California's bats help the ecosystem.

Bats and Plants

Mexican long-tongued bats really do have very long tongues. Their tongues make it easy for them to eat nectar and pollen hidden deep inside agaves and cactus blossoms. As they fly from flower to flower, they carry pollen. Bat pollinators make it possible for new plants to grow. California's deserts bloom, in part, because of bats.

Fruit-eating bats are even more important in the tropics. Major crops like bananas, dates, figs, and vanilla rely on bats for pollination. Without bats, farmers in many countries would have fewer crops to sell.

**A little brown bat
munches on an insect.** ▶

Bats and Bugs

The little brown bat really is little
and brown. Adult little brown bats
are only four inches tall. For such
little animals, they eat an incredible
number of bugs. Their favorite foods
are biting insects like mosquitoes
and midges. Just one little brown bat
can catch and eat 600 mosquitoes
per hour! Mosquitoes can cause
serious diseases. Little brown bats
keep them under control. —*Lisa Jo Rudy*

Joe McDonald/Animals Animals

Curious About Bats?

It's not always easy to find bats, but if you
follow these tips, you might get lucky.

- Look for bats just as the Sun is rising
  or setting.
- Pick an open spot where you can
  see bats' dark wings against the
  lighter sky.
- Look for bats in areas where there
  are plenty of night-flying bugs. Near
  water is best.
- Try watching for bats near lights
  that attract insects. Bats may be
  attracted to the tasty prey.

Remember that bats are important to the
ecosystem. That's why you should never
disturb sleeping or hibernating bats.

**Bats leave their daytime
roost for a night of
insect-hunting.**

Merlin D. Tuttle, Bat Conservation International

Compare/Contrast Writing Frame

Use the Writing Frame below to orally summarize "Pollination and Seed Dispersal."

The process of pollination and seed dispersal are **similar** because

_____ .

In pollination _____

_____ .

Unlike pollination, _____

is the process of spreading seeds. It is **different** than pollination

because _____ .

Seed dispersal and pollination are the **same** because _____

and _____ both can stick to _____ .

However, in seed dispersal the **difference** is that the seeds _____

_____ .

Here they may grow into new plants.

Use the frame to write the summary on another sheet of paper. Be sure to include the **bold** signal words. Keep this as a model of this Text Structure.

Critical Thinking

1. The food animals get from flowers is called _____ .

    A. seeds

    B. pollen

    C. nectar

2. Locate the text in "Bats About Bats" that explains how bats help plants.

3. Find the section in "Bats About Bats" that gives you suggestions on how to find bats.

4. Look at the diagram on page 60. Discuss with a partner how the bird helps with pollination.

Diagrams usually contain labels that help to identify each part.

Digital Learning

For a list of links and activities that relate to this Science standard, visit the California Treasures Web site at www.macmillanmh.com to access the Content Readers resources.

Have children view the Science in Motion "Pollination."

EL In addition, distribute copies of the Translated Concept Summaries in Spanish, Chinese, Hmong, Khmer, and Vietnamese.

Plants as Food and Shelter

Animals depend on plants in many ways. Animals breathe in oxygen that is produced by plants. They depend on plants for food. They also use plants for shelter and protection.

Every part of a plant is food for some animal. Caterpillars and rabbits eat mainly plant leaves. Other animals, such as beetles, eat plant roots and stems. Animals such as earthworms and some snails eat plants that are no longer living. Bears, birds, bats, monkeys, and some lizards eat fruits and seeds.

Even meat eaters depend on plants for food. Remember, plants are the main source of energy entering food chains. Meat eaters depend on plant eaters. Plant eaters depend on plants. Directly or indirectly, all animals need plants for food.

▲ Squirrels use nuts as a source of food energy.

Animals make nests, dens, burrows, and other shelters from plants. Squirrels move into tree holes and line them with soft moss and leaves. Many birds collect twigs and sticks and weave them into a tight nest. Birds use the nests to keep their eggs safe and to care for their young.

An animal senses danger. What can it do? Hide! Leafhoppers and garter snakes hide in the grass for shelter and safety. Rabbit or birds stay out of sight in the bushes. Fish sneak among thick seaweed beads in the ocean. Plants help keep animals safe from harm.

▲ How does the grass help the snake hide from predators? Look at the color of the snake and the grass.

The bird uses twigs and plant materials to build its nest. Nests provide a safe place where birds can feed their young.

Distant Cousins?

Leopards once thought to be related turn out to be from completely different families.

Clouded leopards are medium-size wildcats that live on mainland Southeast Asia and the islands of Borneo and Sumatra. Their name comes from the cloudlike spots that help them hide in the jungle. Because they live alone and like to hide from people, we know very little about clouded leopards. Now, though, we know more.

For more than 100 years, scientists believed that the clouded leopards found in Southeast Asia and on Borneo and Sumatra were the same species. But researchers compared their genes. They found that the two big cats belong to entirely separate species.

▼ **This clouded leopard lives on the islands of Sumatra and Borneo.**

▼ **The mainland clouded leopard is a separate species from its island cousin.**

Home Jungle Home

The forests of Sumatra and Borneo are home to many unique animals and plants. In one recent year, 52 new species were discovered in the tropical rain forest at the center of Borneo. To protect these animals and plants, the governments of the three countries on Borneo agreed to protect the habitat. This agreement will help the clouded leopard survive.

Why a Meat-Eater Needs Plants

Clouded leopards don't eat plants, but without the plants in their rain forest habitat, they could not survive. Every animal is part of a food web that includes other animals as well as plants. All parts of the food web are important, but without plants, it would quickly fall apart.

It starts with energy from the Sun. Plants use the Sun's energy to grow. Squirrels, monkeys, deer, and wild pigs are plant-eaters. They get energy when they eat fruit, berries, grass, leaves, and roots. Then the clouded leopard and other predators eat these plant eaters. The energy passes on to the predators. This flow of energy is what keeps a food web going. The forest's trees are important to clouded leopards in another way. These leopards are the best climbers in the cat family. Up in a tree the clouded leopard waits. When its prey comes by below, the leopard pounces, and dinner is served!

Wayne Lawler/Corbis

▲ The countries on the island of Borneo have agreed to protect the clouded leopard's habitat.

69

Sequence Writing Frame

Use the Writing Frame below to orally summarize "Distant Cousins?"

Every plant and animal in the forest of Sumatra and Borneo is a part of the food web.

It **starts** with _____

_____ .

Plants _____

_____ .

Next animals such as _____

_____ .

Then the clouded leopard _____

_____ .

After that, energy _____

_____ .

This flow of energy is what keeps a food web going.

Use the frame to write the summary on another sheet of paper. Be sure to include the **bold** signal words. Keep this as a model of this Text Structure.

Critical Thinking

1 Many animals depend on plants for shelter and _____.

    A. pollination

    B. seed dispersal

    C. food

2 Point to the place in the text "Plants as Food and Shelter" that mentions how animals depend on plants for shelter.

3 Find the sentence in "Distant Cousins?" that describes the clouded leopard's camouflage.

4 Look at the globe on page 68. Why is it important to the article "Distant Cousins?"

An inset map is an enlargement of a small section of the map.

Digital Learning

For a list of links and activities that relate to this Science standard, visit the California Treasures Web site at www.macmillanmh.com to access the Content Readers resources.

Have children view the e-Review "Living Things Need Each Other."

EL In addition, distribute copies of the Translated Concept Summaries in Spanish, Chinese, Hmong, Khmer, and Vietnamese.

Science

Macmillan/McGraw-Hill

Mighty Microorganisms

You cannot see them, but there are tiny living things every place you look. They are on the food you eat. They are on the book you are holding now. They are inside and outside your body. You will find them in oceans, lakes, ponds, and rivers. You will even find them in puddles.

What are these tiny creatures? They are microorganisms (migh•kroh•AWR•guh•niz•uhmz). **Microorganisms** are living things too small to be seen with just our eyes. Many microorganisms are made of only one cell (SEL). **Cells** are the smallest units of life. Plants and animals are made of many cells.

Most microorganisms can be seen through a tool called a microscope. A microscope shows an enlarged view of an object. Many classroom microscopes magnify objects 30 to 60 times their normal size.

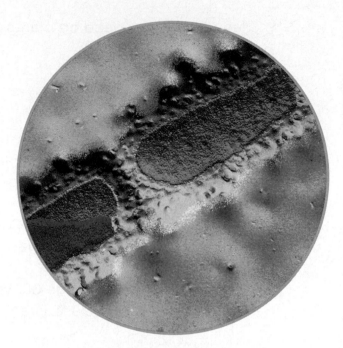

▲ Escherichia coli

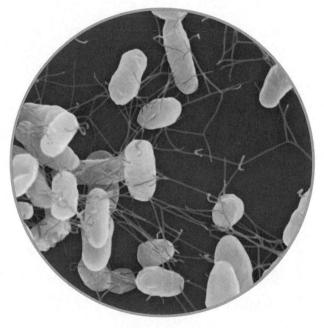

▲ Salmonella

There are many kinds of microorganisms. One of the smallest is called **bacteria** (bak•TEER•ee•uh). Bacteria can be both helpful and harmful to human life. Harmful bacteria can cause illness. Helpful bacteria aid humans in swallowing and digesting food. They can even help to fight disease.

Protists (PROH•tists) are another group of microorganisms. Like bacteria, some protists can be helpful or harmful. Some protists eat bacteria. This helps to keep harmful bacteria under control. Other protists cause disease. Many harmful protists are found in ponds and lakes.

How do protists compare to bacteria? They are much larger than bacteria. They also have structures that do special jobs. They have parts for making and using food. They even have parts for making new protists.

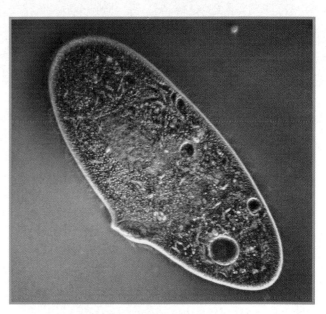

▲ This photo shows what a protist looks like under a microscope.

Do Your Part to Prevent Disease

We can do a lot to keep harmful microorganisms out of our bodies. This chart shows how people can stay healthy from diseases caused by microorganisms.

Disease	Microorganism	Prevention
tooth decay	tooth bacteria	Brush and floss to remove food.
Lyme disease	bacteria in ticks	Wear long pants on hikes.
dysentery	amoeba-like protist	Drink clean water.
malaria	protist in mosquitos	Use anti-malaria medicine.
food poisoning	salmonella bacteria	Cook and handle food properly.

Meet the
"GOOD GERMS"

Some germs have a bad reputation they don't deserve.

"Wash your hands. They're covered with germs!" How many times a day do you hear this? It's good advice, but it turns out that not all germs are bad germs.

Germs are really tiny living things called bacteria and viruses. Bacteria can cause terrible diseases. They can also be very helpful. In fact, you have hundreds of different kinds of bacteria in your body right now. They're helping you to break down the food you eat into useful nutrients.

Good Germs Against Bad Germs

Doctors use medicines called antibiotics to kill off bad germs. Antibiotics, though, can cause diarrhea and upset stomachs. Now nutritionists say that good germs called probiotics can actually help your body handle the antibiotics. They can also help your body fight diarrhea.

Even more impressive, good germs can help your body fight some diseases. That's because probiotics make the body's defenses even stronger. When bad germs attack, you can fight them off more easily with extra probiotics. One disease, called rotavirus, attacks children all over the world. Probiotics can be used to fight rotavirus.

◀ A microscopic view of a type of "good" germ

Probiotics can help kids who are taking medicine for strep throat.

Germs Made Especially for Kids

Kids get a lot of bacterial infections, such as earaches and strep throat. Doctors prescribe antibiotics to treat those infections. Kids, though, are especially likely to get diarrhea and upset stomach from antibiotics. Researchers have found that probiotics can really help kids to feel better while they're taking antibiotics.

Eat Your Tasty Germs!

Probiotics do come in pills. But there are easier, tastier ways to get your good germs! Probiotics are a natural part of yogurt, buttermilk, and other milk products. —*Lisa Jo Rudy*

Milk products such as yogurt contain "good" germs. ▶

Compare/Contrast Writing Frame

Use the Writing Frame below to orally summarize "Mighty Microorganisms."

Bacteria and protists are **both** _____.

They are the **same** because they are **both** _____

_____.

Helpful bacteria can _____

_____.

Harmful bacteria can _____.

Like bacteria, some protists _____.
However, protists **differ** from bacteria in many ways.

One difference is that some protists _____

_____.

Another difference is _____.

Protists are also **different** because they have _____

_____.

Use the frame to write the summary on another sheet of paper.
Be sure to include the **bold** signal words. Keep this as a model of
this Text Structure.

Critical Thinking

1 Microorganism that can be found in water are called _____ .

   A. protists

   B. producers

   C. bacteria

2 Find the sentence in "Meet the 'Good Germs' " that gives you a definition of probiotics.

3 What happens when antibiotics kill off bad germs? Find the section in "Meet the 'Good Germs' " that gives you the answer.

4 Is there information in the chart on page 73 that is not in the text? Discuss with a partner.

A chart has columns and rows. Some charts are read down the columns, while others are read across rows.

Digital Learning

For a list of links and activities that relate to this Science standard, visit the California Treasures Web site at www.macmillanmh.com to access the Content Readers resources.

Have children view the e-Review "Microorganisms."

EL In addition, distribute copies of the Translated Concept Summaries in Spanish, Chinese, Hmong, Khmer, and Vietnamese.

Minerals

All rocks are made up of natural, nonliving substances called **minerals** (MIN•uh•ruhlz). Minerals are identified by physical properties such as color, luster, streak, cleavage, and hardness.

Luster describes the way light reflects off the surface of a mineral. Some minerals have a metallic, or shiny, luster. Others may be dull, while others may be glassy.

Cleavage (KLEE•vij) is the way a mineral splits. Some minerals, like mica (MIGH•kuh), split along a flat surface into a thin sheet. Other minerals, like quartz, split apart unevenly.

Streak is the color of the powder left when a mineral is scratched along a white tile called a streak plate. Some minerals leave a streak that is the same color as the mineral itself. Other minerals leave a different streak color.

Hardness is a property that refers to a mineral's ability to scratch another mineral or be scratched by another mineral. The **Moh's Hardness Scale** shows the hardness of a few common minerals. Diamond, 10 on the scale, is the hardest mineral. Talc, 1 on the scale, is one of the softest minerals. There are more minerals for each level of hardness.

▲ Pyrite, often called fool's gold, has a metallic luster.

▲ Hematite leaves a reddish streak, as shown on this streak plate.

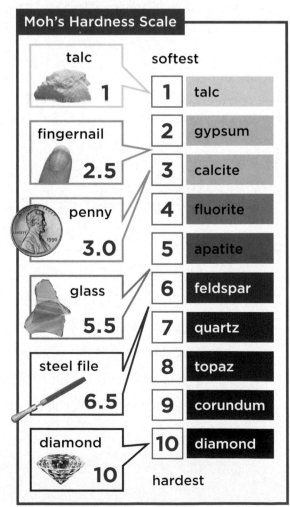

Moh's Hardness Scale

talc **1**	softest
	1 talc
fingernail **2.5**	**2** gypsum
	3 calcite
penny **3.0**	**4** fluorite
	5 apatite
glass **5.5**	**6** feldspar
	7 quartz
steel file **6.5**	**8** topaz
	9 corundum
diamond **10**	**10** diamond
	hardest

Different processes that take place on Earth form different kinds of rocks. Igneous rocks form when melted rock cools and hardens above or below the ground. The word *igneous* means "made by fire."

Some rocks are formed by tiny particles called **sediments**. Some sediments are tiny particles of rocks and minerals. Other sediments are bits of plants, bones, shells, or other animal materials.

Most sedimentary rocks form when sediments settle into layers. Over time the layers change to rock.

Extreme heat and pressure can cause any kind of rock to change to metamorphic rock. Did you know that over time all rocks change from one form to another? The cycle by which rocks change from one form to another is called **the rock cycle**.

The Rock Cycle

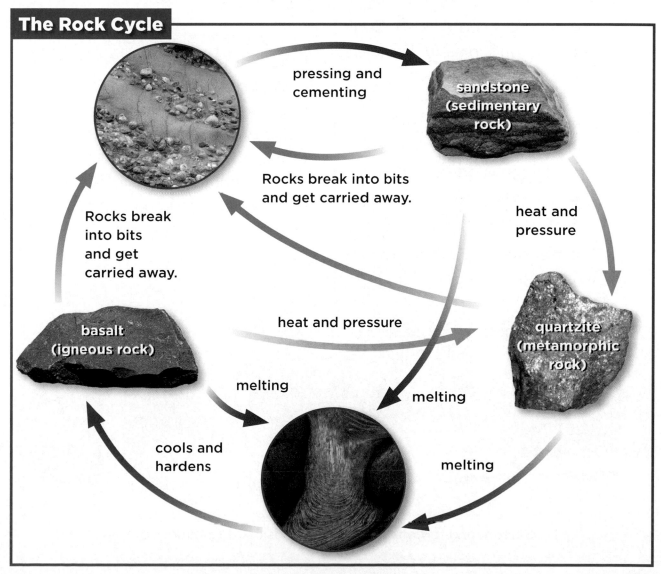

pressing and cementing

sandstone (sedimentary rock)

Rocks break into bits and get carried away.

Rocks break into bits and get carried away.

heat and pressure

basalt (igneous rock)

heat and pressure

quartzite (metamorphic rock)

melting

melting

cools and hardens

melting

A Computer in a Grain of Sand

Rocks are broken down by natural forces until they are grains of sand. Humans have found a good use for nature's product.

When you take a walk on the beach, you're crunching future computer chips. That's because silicon, an element commonly found in sand, is the most important ingredient in computer chips. Why? The best materials for making computer chips are called semiconductors, of which silicon is one example. Semiconductors allow just a little electricity to pass through.

That's perfect for the switches inside computer chips. Silicon is almost as easy to find as oxygen, the gas that's part of the air we breathe.

Most sand starts out as rock. Erosion by wind, water, and other rocks gradually breaks huge boulders down into smaller pieces. This process continues over thousands of years, until the pieces become grains of sand. Now humans are changing sand even further by turning it into computer chips.

Jupiter Images/Goodshot/Alamy

Silicon, an element found in sand, is used to make computer chips.

Making Computer Chips

Computer chips start with a scoop of sand. The sand is heated in a furnace to produce pure silicon. The silicon is turned into long rods, about 7 inches wide. The rods are sliced into thin wafers.

Meanwhile, engineers design the computer's circuits. Circuits are metal paths along which electricity flows. Switches in the circuits turn the flow of electricity on and off. Computer chips are very tiny, so the engineers design their circuits on huge pieces of paper. Then they shrink their designs.

When the designs have been shrunk to about half-inch squares, engineers etch the circuit designs onto silicon wafers. Metal is laid over the etched circuits. Another silicon wafer is placed on top of the metal circuits. Another circuit design is etched onto the second silicon wafer. This process is repeated many times. Finally metal circuits are added to the very top layers of the silicon-and-circuit sandwich.

Now engineers use a laser beam to cut the many-layered silicon-and-circuit sandwich into tiny computer chips. Depending on the circuit design, the computer chips may be used for office work, games, or even making music. —*Lisa Jo Rudy*

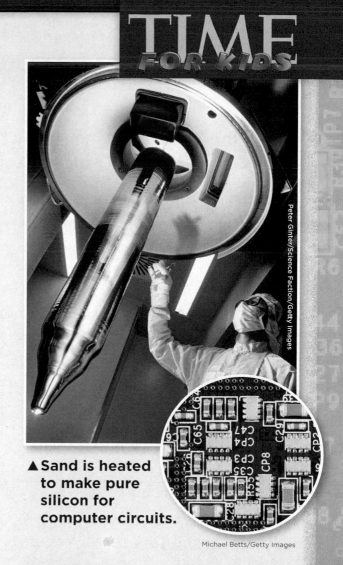

Peter Ginter/Science Faction/Getty Images

▲ **Sand is heated to make pure silicon for computer circuits.**

Michael Betts/Getty Images

Erin Patrice O'Brien/Getty Images

John Foxx/Getty Images

◄ **Many modern devices use silicon chips.**

Sequence Writing Frame

Use the Writing Frame below to orally summarize "A Computer in a Grain of Sand."

Making computer chips is a long process. Computer chips **start** with

_____

that is _____ .

After that the pure silicon is _____ .

Meanwhile engineers _____

by etching _____ .

Then metal _____ .

This process is repeated many times. **Finally** metal circuits are added to the very top layers of the silicon-and-circuit sandwich.

After that, engineers _____

_____ .

Depending on the circuit design, the computer chips may be used for office work, games, or even making music.

Use the frame to write the summary on another sheet of paper. Be sure to include the **bold** signal words. Keep this as a model of this Text Structure.

Critical Thinking

1 The way a mineral splits or breaks along flat surfaces is called
_____ .

    A. streak

    B. cleavage

    C. hardness

2 Is silicon easy to find? Point to the sentence in "A Computer in a Grain of Sand" that answers this question.

3 Discover the phrase on page 79 that defines the process by which rocks change from one form to another.

4 Review the Moh's Hardness Scale on page 78. Can a fingernail scratch glass? Discuss with a partner.

Charts present information in a simple and organized way.

Digital Learning

For a list of links and activities that relate to this Science standard, visit the California Treasures Web site at www.macmillanmh.com to access the Content Readers resources.

Have children view the e-Review "Minerals: The Building Blocks of Rocks."

EL In addition, distribute copies of the Translated Concept Summaries in Spanish, Chinese, Hmong, Khmer, and Vietnamese.

Slow Changes to Landforms

Natural features on Earth's surface are called **landforms**. Some landforms change in a short period of time—sometimes hours. A mudslide quickly changes a hillside, for example. Most landforms, however, change over extremely long periods of time.

▲ Wave action will eventually erode this cliff in Cabo San Lucas, Mexico.

Landforms can be reshaped by water, waves, wind, and ice. Rainfall that does not soak into the ground flows downhill. It flows from the tops of mountains to the sea. As it flows, the water forms a channel in the ground. The water flows into streams and rivers. As the rivers move downhill, they cut away land along their sides and carry away sediments. This cutting away of the land forms a **valley**. Running water changes the land along the sides and bottoms of streams and rivers. A river may eventually empty into an ocean. At the place it meets the ocean, the river runs even more slowly. It drops sediments that have been carried for miles to the mouth of the river. The sediments form an area of land called a **delta**.

The force of waves changes a beach. The powerful force of waves can change rocky cliffs. The constant action of waves breaks large chunks of rock from the bottom of the cliff. This slowly makes the rocky cliffs smaller. Waves can also pick up tons of sand. The sand can be deposited somewhere else. The size of a beach may shrink in one place, but grow in another. During a storm, powerful winds cause large waves. The waves can wash away much of a beach in just a few hours.

Wind changes the land by acting like a sandblaster. Wind carrying sand and bits of rock scratches the surface of rocks like sandpaper. This causes small bits of rock to break off. Then the wind picks up the new bits and carries them away. The erosion of rocks by wind takes many, many years. Wind can blow sand into hills called **sand dunes**. Sand dunes are formed by particles of sand that are picked up by wind. As dry sand blows, objects such as rocks or grasses block it. The movement of the sand particles is slowed by the objects. A sand dune begins to take shape.

On colder parts of Earth, large, thick sheets of ice called **glaciers** (GLAY•shuhrz) slowly creep over the land. Millions of years ago, glaciers covered much of Earth.

Glaciers are formed in cold areas where more snow falls than can melt. The thick snow slowly changes into ice. It's bottom becomes fluid like. The sheet of ice begins to flow downhill. The ice at the bottom and sides of a glacier freezes onto rocks. As the glacier continues to move, it tears the rocks right from the ground. The glacier tears rocks from the sides of a valley as well. Sometimes rocks the size of a house are torn up and moved. A glacier widens, deepens, and leaves a U- shaped valley behind.

A glacier leaves a U-shaped valley behind, like the one shown here in White River National Forest, Colorado.

85

Vanishing Alaska

Vincent J. Musi/Aurora

What's happening to an Alaska village may hold lessons for much bigger cities.

Shishmaref is a tiny village in Alaska. Little by little, its traditional way of life is disappearing. Over the past 35 years, the village has lost between 100 and 300 feet of its coastline. Half of that has been lost since 1997. Shishmaref may become a victim of global warming.

A Disappearing Life

Shishmaref is so remote that no road connects it to the outside world. The town has 10 dog teams. Walrus-tusk carving is taught in school, and so is the Inupiaq language.

Shishmaref is surrounded by natural beauty and natural resources. People there still get much of their food from hunting and fishing.

But up and down Alaska's coast, people worry that the animals and fish they live on will disappear.

"We are at a crossroads," the mayor of one Alaskan town says. "Is it practical to stand and fight our Mother Ocean? Or do we surrender and move?"

▼ Kids in Shishmaref witness the effects of global warming every day.

Vincent J. Musi/Aurora

Al Grillo/AP Photo

Stay and Fight, or Move Away?

Already, Shishmaref is melting into the ocean. The sea ice is thinning. Houses are collapsing. Giant waves have washed away the school playground. Should Eskimo people move their villages inland to escape the rising sea? The idea is gathering support. The people of Shishmaref reluctantly voted to move to a site called Tin Creek, 12 miles away. It was a very difficult decision.

▲ **Shishmaref is melting into the ocean.**

One Eskimo mother who is also a town leader explained, "Shishmaref is where it is because of what the ocean, rivers, streams, and the land provide to us. We are hunters, and we are gatherers. We have been here for countless generations. We value our way of life. It provides for our very existence."

What's the Best Choice for the Future?

Moving Shishmaref to a more protected location could be outrageously expensive. The U.S. Army Corps of Engineers thinks it would cost about $1 million for each resident. Shishmaref's villagers, though, want to stay together.

▼ **Village leaders worry about losing their traditional way of life.**

If global warming ever begins washing away coastal towns in the rest of the United States, the cost of relocating everyone is almost impossible to imagine. Will more villages of Alaska move inland? Will the communities be broken up? Will the United States government pay out millions to try to save the towns or move them? The choices made for Shishmaref and other Alaskan villages will become a model for other, much bigger cities in the United States. —*Margot Roosevelt*

Vincent J. Musi/Aurora

Description Writing Frame

Use the Writing Frame below to orally summarize "Slow Changes to Landforms."

Natural features on Earth's surface are called landforms. Landforms can change in **many interesting ways**.

One interesting way landforms are changed is by water. As the rivers

journey downhill, they _____.

Rivers can also create a delta by _____.

Waves can also change landforms. **For example**, waves _____

_____.

Another interesting way landforms are changed is by the wind. For

example, wind carrying _____.

The erosion of rocks by wind takes many years. Wind can also _____

_____.

Ice such as _____ can also change landforms in

interesting ways. When glaciers move, they _____

_____. This movement can widen, deepen, and leave a U-shaped valley behind.

Use the frame to write the summary on another sheet of paper. Be sure to include the **bold** signal words. Keep this as a model of this Text Structure.

Critical Thinking

1 Landforms can be reshaped by water, waves, ice, and

_____ .

    A. wind

    B. sun

    C. sand

2 Find the sentence in "Vanishing Alaska" that explains why Shishmaref is disappearing.

3 Point to the place in "Slow Changes to Landforms" that gives an example of a quick way landforms are changed.

4 Select your favorite photo from "Vanishing Alaska." Orally create a new caption for it.

Captions help the reader tell the difference between images that may seem quite similar at first glance.

Digital Learning

For a list of links and activities that relate to this Science standard, visit the California Treasures Web site at www.macmillanmh.com to access the Content Readers resources.

Have children view the e-Review "Landforms: Changing Over Time."

EL In addition, distribute copies of the Translated Concept Summaries in Spanish, Chinese, Hmong, Khmer, and Vietnamese.

Weathering

Rocks are constantly changing. Freezing and thawing, plants, wind, and pressure can cause rocks to break into smaller pieces. The breakdown of rocks is called **weathering** (WE•thuhr•ing).

In **chemical weathering**, rocks break down due to chemical changes to the minerals. Oxygen, acids, and carbon dioxide can react with minerals in rock and cause chemical weathering.

Physical weathering happens when things such as wind and rain break down rocks. Physical weathering causes rocks to simply change size and shape. The chemicals they are made of do not change. Here are some of the things that cause physical weathering.

▲ Hematite contains iron. Things with iron can rust and break down when the iron mixes with oxygen.

North Window Arch in Arches National Park, Utah, was formed by physical weathering. ▼

These roots will eventually split the rock apart.

Freezing and Thawing

Water from rain or melted snow enters small cracks in rocks. If the water freezes, it expands, or takes up more space. This causes cracks to widen. Later the water may thaw, or melt. Over time, repeated freezing and thawing breaks rocks apart.

Plants

A plant's roots can force their way through small cracks in rocks. As the roots grow larger, they cause the cracks to widen and the rocks to break apart.

Exfoliation

Some buried rocks, like granite, are changed when heavy layers of rock wear away. The outer layers of the once-buried granite expand more than its lower layers. This causes the outer layers of rock to peel off like the layers of an onion. This kind of physical weathering is called exfoliation (eks•foh•lee•AY•suhn).

Abrasion

Winds can also change rock. Winds that carry bits of sand can break down the softer parts of rocks. The sharp edges of sand wear away rocks. This wearing away of rocks by blowing sand is called wind abrasion (uh•BRAY•zhuhn).

The Old Man of the Mountain

A much-loved natural sculpture teaches an important lesson about the forces that shape Earth's surface.

Library of Congress

▲ In the 1930s, tourists gaze up at the Old Man of the Mountain.

The Old Man of the Mountain was just a rock formation in Franconia Notch, New Hampshire. But to many people, he was an old friend. The Old Man of the Mountain appeared to be a face, seen from the side, carved out of solid rock. From chin to forehead, the face measured 40 feet. It was 25 feet wide.

Every year thousands of people would visit Franconia Notch just to say hello to the Old Man. He became so popular that in 1945 he was named the state symbol of New Hampshire. In 2000, the New Hampshire quarter issued by the U.S. Mint featured the Old Man.

A 12,000-Year-Old Man

The story of the Old Man of the Mountain starts about 12,000 years ago, during the last ice age. Back then, an ice sheet covered North America. As the ice sheet melted, it created the mountains that became Franconia Notch and carved the Old Man.

In 1805 some surveyors claimed to be the first to see the face. In fact, though, even in the 1600s, American Indians told stories of the mountain with a stone face.

▼ **Native Americans first noticed the Old Man's profile.**

David Noble Photography/Alamy

The End of the Old Man

Even as thousands of people were visiting and admiring the Old Man of the Mountain, natural forces were destroying it.

◀ In 2003, the granite slabs collapsed and the Old Man was gone.

The Old Man was made of five slabs of granite. Behind its chin was a long, narrow cavern. That meant that just about 2 feet of the chin was actually connected to the cliff. It was held there by the weight of the other four slabs of granite. It was an amazing balancing act!

Through the years, rain and snow blew into the cavern and other cracks between the five slabs. The water between the slabs froze and expanded, pushing them apart. This happened again and again for thousands of years.

Finally, on May 3, 2003, the rock just behind the Old Man of the Mountain's chin moved slightly. When that happened, the chin fell down the cliff. The rest of the Old Man fell almost immediately afterward.

Remembering the Old Man

Even today, people come to the park to remember it. An online scrapbook is filled with memories and pictures of the Old Man. —*Lisa Jo Rudy*

Nature's Sculptures

Examples of sculptures carved by natural forces can be seen around the world. Here are two examples in the United States.

Half Dome, Yosemite National Park, California: This granite dome rises more than 4,700 feet above the Yosemite Valley. According to Indian legend, the dome shows the face of an Indian girl.

Arches National Park, Utah: The many rock formations in this high desert area are made of sandstone. They have been carved by wind, water, and other forces over millions of years.

Problem/Solution Writing Frame

Use the Writing Frame below to orally summarize "The Old Man of the Mountain."

The forces of nature destroyed the Old Man of the Mountain rock formation in Franconia Notch, New Hampshire.

This is a problem because many people _____

_____ .

This problem occurred because _____

_____ .

To help solve the problem, Franconia State Park _____

_____ .

There is also an _____

_____ .

The result is that people can enjoy the Old Man of the Mountain for years to come.

Use the frame to write the summary on another sheet of paper. Be sure to include the **bold** signal words. Keep this as a model of this Text Structure.

Critical Thinking

1 Abrasion, exfoliation and freezing are all examples
   of _____.

   A. weathering

   B. chemical weathering

   C. physical weathering

2 Locate the section in "The Old Man of the Mountain" that
   explains how the rock formation was created.

3 Find the word in "Weathering" that explains the process that
   causes the outer layers of rock to peel.

4 Look at the picture at the top of page 93. Discuss
   the impact of weathering on the mountain with
   a partner.

Photographs provide
visual examples of facts
or ideas that appear in
a text.

Digital Learning

For a list of links and activities that relate to this Science standard,
visit the California Treasures Web site at www.macmillanmh.com
to access the Content Readers resources.

Have children view the e-Review "Weathering."

EL In addition, distribute copies of the Translated Concept
Summaries in Spanish, Chinese, Hmong, Khmer, and Vietnamese.

CALIFORNIA IN THE WORLD

You can describe a place in many ways. You can tell what the weather is like in a place. You can take a photograph of a place. You can even tell a place by its street address.

How might you describe the location of California? You could say that California has a "global address," or an address on Earth. California's global address is that it is part of the United States. The United States has a global address too. It is part of a continent, or large piece of land, called North America. Can you find North America on the map?

Even North America has a global address. It is part of the Western Hemisphere. A **hemisphere** is half of a sphere. Earth is divided into four hemispheres. They are the Northern, Southern, Eastern, and Western Hemispheres.

The Western Hemisphere

ARCTIC OCEAN

NORTH AMERICA

UNITED STATES

CALIFORNIA

ATLANTIC OCEAN

PACIFIC OCEAN

SOUTH AMERICA

N
W   E
S

0	1,500	3,000 miles
0	1,500	3,000 kilometers

Every place on Earth has a global address based on its location. To describe the address of a place, geographers use maps with grids. **Grids** are lines that cross on a map. The grid system is based on two sets of lines called **latitude** and **longitude**.

Lines of latitude measure how far north or south a place is from the equator. Lines of latitude are also called **parallels**. Parallels north of the equator are labeled "N." Parallels south of the equator are labeled "S."

Lines of longitude measure distance east or west. Lines of longitude are also called **meridians**. The prime meridian is the starting place for measuring distance from east to west. Meridians east of the prime meridian are labeled "E." Meridians west of the prime meridian are labeled "W."

Lines of latitude and longitude measure distance in **degrees**. The equator is 0 degrees. The symbol for degrees is °.

California: Latitude and Longitude

California's National Parks

NATIONAL PARK SERVICE

California's diverse geography is home to spectacular national parks.

California is a big state, stretching 770 miles from north to south. That's almost 10 degrees of latitude on the globe. A state this long is bound to have lots of geographic diversity. One indication of that is the number and variety of national parks in California.

National parks are areas set aside by the U. S. government because they are especially beautiful, important, or unique.

California's National Parks:

- Channel Islands National Park
- Death Valley National Park
- Joshua Tree National Park
- Lassen Volcanic National Park
- Point Reyes National Seashore
- Redwood National Park
- Sequoia & Kings Canyon National Parks
- Yosemite National Park

Here are profiles of two of California's magnificent national parks.

Redwoods
Lava Beds
Lassen
Point Reyes
Yosemite
Sequoia & Kings Canyon
Death Valley
Channel Islands
Joshua Tree

Joe Lemonnier

Sharing the Latitude

California's capital, Sacramento, sits just above 38°N latitude. If you traveled due east from Sacramento all the way around the world, you would pass through or near these cities: Washington, D.C.; Lisbon, Portugal; Ankara, Turkey; Tianjin, China; and Pyongyang, North Korea.

Lassen Volcanic National Park

In northeastern California, in a town called Mineral, is Lassen Volcanic National Park. Lassen Peak is the largest of a group of more than 30 volcanoes in the park. It last erupted in 1915, spewing ash for 200 miles. Scientists check the volcanoes for signs of new eruptions.

Where there are volcanoes, there's lava. Here, the lava is just below the surface. All that heat creates roaring fumaroles (steam and volcanic-gas vents), thumping mud pots, boiling pools, and steaming ground. The steam comes from water that's heated by underground lava.

Joshua Tree National Park

Joshua Tree National Park is in the high desert in southern California. If you drive by it, you see very little. If you go into the huge park, though, you can discover an amazing variety of plants and animals. If you explore the land, you'll be amazed at the strange shapes of the rocks and sand formed by wind and rain. If you wander around the park at night, you'll see thousands of stars in the sky.

Joshua Tree National Park is best known for its namesake, the Joshua tree. The leaves of the twisted, spiky tree were used by American Indians to make baskets and sandals. The seeds and nuts were roasted for food. —*Lisa Jo Rudy*

Altrendo Travel/Getty Images

▲ **Lassen has boiling pools and steaming vents.**

▼ **The Joshua tree thrives in the high desert.**

Altrendo Panoramic/Getty Images

Description Writing Frame

Use the Writing Frame below to orally summarize "California's National Parks."

California's national parks have **many interesting features**.

One feature of the National Parks is the volcanoes at

_____ .

In 1915 _____ .

Another interesting feature of Lassen park is the roaring

_____ .

The steam comes from _____

_____ .

There are many interesting trees in California's National Parks.

For example, the twisted, spiky _____

was used by _____

_____ .

To see one, just visit _____
in Southern California.

Use the frame to write the summary on another sheet of paper. Be sure to include the **bold** signal words. Keep this as a model of this Text Structure.

Critical Thinking

1. Lines that cross one another on a map are called _____.

   A. grids

   B. latitude

   C. longitude

2. Find the sentence in "California's National Parks" that explains what a fumarole is.

3. Point to the place in "California in the World" that gives an example of how you might describe the location of California.

4. Review the map on page 97. Find the longitude and latitude that is closest to where you live.

> A compass rose shows where the cardinal and intermediate directions are on the map.

Digital Learning

For a list of links and activities that relate to this History/Social Science standard, visit the California Treasures Web site at www.macmillanmh.com to access the Content Readers resources. Have children visit the Field Trip "Yosemite National Park."

CALIFORNIA'S PHYSICAL REGIONS

California has four physical regions: mountains, valleys, coasts, and deserts. Each unique region affects human activity in different ways.

Mountains

Mountains can be found in every part of California. They are the most common landform in the state and cover more than half the land.

People have always traveled to California's highest mountain ranges to experience the beautiful landscape. The mountains also supply important natural resources such as water, wood, and minerals. Major **industries** grew up around these resources. An industry is all the businesses that make one kind of good or provide one kind of service.

Tourism is an important industry in California. **Tourists** are people who travel for the fun of seeing new sights. Tourists from all over the world visit California's mountains to enjoy outdoor activities such as skiing, snowboarding, hiking, and boating.

Valleys

California's Central Valley is one of the biggest **valleys** in the world. A valley is a low area between mountains.

The Central Valley is in the middle of four different mountain ranges. It is formed from two valleys, the Sacramento Valley in the north and the San Joaquin Valley in the south.

Many people have come to the Central Valley because of its most valuable natural resource, **fertile** land. Fertile land has rich soil that produces crops easily.

California: Mountain Region

- ■ Mountain region
- ★ State capital
- ● Other city
- ▲ Mountain peak

KLAMOUTH MTS.
CASCADE RANGE
Mount Shasta
MODOC PLATEAU
Eureka
Redding
Lassen Peak
COAST RANGES
SIERRA NEVADA
Lake Tahoe
Sacramento
Mono Lake
San Francisco
San José
Fresno
Mount Whitney
COAST RANGES
Bakersfield
Mount Pinos
Santa Barbara
TRANSVERSE RANGES
San Bernardino
Los Angeles
PACIFIC OCEAN
PENINSULAR RANGES
San Diego
MEXICO

0   75   150 miles
0   75   150 kilometers

Today, the Central Valley is one of the world's most productive agricultural regions. **Agriculture** (AG•rih•kul•chur) is the business of growing crops and raising animals.

The Coast

Close to three out of four people in California live in the coastal region. Many live near the mountains of the Coast Ranges. Others have settled in the coastal plains of Southern California.

Californians enjoy the warm and pleasant climate of the coast. They also enjoy the ocean. The ocean supports important industries, such as tourism. Millions of tourists flock to California's beautiful coast and beaches every year. Fishing is another important coastal industry. California fishing boats catch much of the salmon, crab, and other seafood that we eat. California's coastal cities are centers of international business. Ships from all over the world dock in their harbors.

Desert Regions

California's desert region is made up of three deserts: the Colorado Desert, the Mojave Desert, and the Great Basin. California's deserts sometimes have no rain for months.

A desert region can also be very hot. Summer temperatures in the desert region are usually over 100 degrees Fahrenheit. However, in the winter the temperature often falls below freezing.

In the 1800s few people lived in California's deserts. There was little rain and few bodies of water. People struggled to find enough water to survive.

Now, thanks to **technology**, things have changed. Technology is the use of skills, tools, and machinery to meet people's needs. One product of technology is **irrigation**. Irrigation is the use of ditches and pipes to bring water to dry land. The Imperial Valley, part of the Colorado Desert, became fertile once it was irrigated. Melons, lettuce, corn, and other fruits and vegetables are now grown there.

Technology makes it possible for people to live, work, and play in very hot places. Today, thousands travel to the California deserts each year to enjoy golf and relaxation.

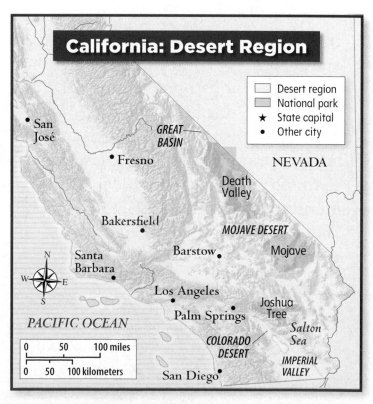

California: Desert Region

Legend:
- Desert region
- National park
- ★ State capital
- • Other city

San José · Fresno · GREAT BASIN · NEVADA · Death Valley · Bakersfield · MOJAVE DESERT · Santa Barbara · Barstow · Mojave · Los Angeles · Palm Springs · Joshua Tree · PACIFIC OCEAN · COLORADO DESERT · Salton Sea · IMPERIAL VALLEY · San Diego

0 50 100 miles
0 50 100 kilometers

Death Valley Vacation

A bike trek through Death Valley

SCPhotos/Alamy

A vacation in a place like this is for people who like extremes.

Death Valley National Park is California's largest national park. It's also one of the most dramatic places on Earth. Its 3.3 million hot, dry acres attract 1 million visitors a year. Why? One reason is that Death Valley offers a lot of extremes.

White Gold

In the 1800s, people came to Death Valley to make their fortunes. But gold, silver, and copper mining did not last long. The real treasure was known as white gold. This was borax, a mineral compound used in cleaning products. Borax is usually found underground. In Death Valley it could be scraped off the surface of rocks.

Today the natural beauty of Death Valley draws visitors for other reasons. Hiking trails and roads let them see stunning landforms.

Sand Dunes Near Stovepipe Wells

Desert winds deposited grains of mountain quartz here. The grains began as solid rock. The dunes and flat sands cover 15 square miles.

Devil's Golf Course

Wind and rain carve salt into amazing pointed shapes called pinnacles. The salt comes from ancient saltwater lakes. The pinnacles grow about one inch every 35 years.

Courtesy Death Valley National Park

Borax was hauled out of Death Valley by mule train.

Badwater Basin

Here is the lowest place in all of North America, 282 feet below sea level. The water is undrinkable, which explains the name.

Undrinkable water gives Badwater its name.

Michael Szönyi/imagebroker/Alamy

Ubehebe Crater

This crater is over a half a mile wide and 770 feet deep. It was formed 4,000 years ago, when magma (hot, liquid rock from under Earth's crust) rose up into cold, shallow groundwater. The mixture turned to steam and exploded. It blew off a massive lid of rock.

The mixture of hot magma and cold water exploded, causing the crater.

Terry Wall/Alamy

Artist's Drive

Along Artist's Drive in the Black Mountains, minerals give the volcanic rocks amazing colors. Iron provides reds, pinks, and yellows. Mica colors rocks mint green. Manganese supplies purple. —*Susan Moger*

Minerals give volcanic rocks their colors.

Michael Szönyi/imagebroker/Alamy

Artis/Riedts/Alamy

Death Valley's Mysterious Moving Rocks

In a dry basin called Racetrack Playa, rocks are on the move. Some are big—705 pounds. Some are small. Behind many of the rocks are long grooves in the dirt. It looks like the stones moved and left tracks. But no one has ever seen them in motion!

Problem/Solution Writing Frame

Use the Writing Frame below to orally summarize "California's Physical Regions."

California has four physical regions: _____

_____.

California's deserts sometimes have no rain for months. In the

past **this was a problem because** _____

_____.

Today there is irrigation. **The result is** _____

_____.

A desert region can also be very hot. Summer temperatures _____

_____.

In the past **this was a problem because** _____

_____.

Today people use technology to beat the heat. **The result** is that

people can _____.

Use the frame to write the summary on another sheet of paper. Be sure to include the **bold** signal words. Keep this as a model of this Text Structure.

Critical Thinking

1 A low area between mountains is a _____ .

   A. coast

   B. desert

   C. valley

2 Point to the word in "California's Physical Regions" for people who travel for the fun of seeing new sights.

3 Locate the section in "Death Valley Vacation" that explains what white gold is.

4 Orally create a caption for your favorite photo in "Death Valley Vacation." Share your caption with a partner.

Photographs provide visual examples of facts or ideas that appear in a text.

Digital Learning

For a list of links and activities that relate to this History/Social Science standard, visit the California Treasures Web site at www.macmillanmh.com to access the Content Readers resources. Have children view the video "The Golden State–Our Home."

LAND MEETS WATER

Californian's coastline stretches almost 1,300 miles from Oregon in the north to Mexico in the south. Although narrow, this land next to the Pacific Ocean is California's most crowded region.

The coast of California varies greatly. In Northern California, some of the mountains come straight to the water's edge. The coast is often rocky and the water can be dangerous. In Southern California, the coastal plain is between the mountains and the ocean. This is a place to visit sand beaches.

Southern California is warm all year round. There is also little rain in the region.

Many Southern Californians spend their free time outside. Surfing, sailing, biking, and beach volleyball are a few of the outdoor activities that residents enjoy.

Southern California is more than fun in the sun. Two very large cities are located along the southern coast. San Diego and Los Angeles are two of the ten largest cities in the United States by population. These cities have major businesses, restaurants, and museums that make them exciting places to live or visit.

Birds such as this puffin can be found along California's coast. ▶

Avalon harbor on Santa Catalina island ▼

The Bay Area, or the region around San Francisco Bay, is home to the largest number of people on the northern coast. There are several large cities in the Bay Area. The Bay Area's Silicon Valley is a famous center of the computer industry.

In the valleys north of San Francisco, the climate is good for growing grapes. Even farther north, the coast is rugged. Thick groves of evergreen forests grow there, and logging, or cutting down trees for their wood, is a major industry.

California's coast is not just famous for its natural beauty and relaxing lifestyle. It is also famous for its earthquakes. An **earthquake** is a shaking of the earth.

Do you know what causes earthquakes? Earth's surface is made up of huge **plates**. These plates are always grinding against one another. Sometimes two plates slip or slide quickly against each other. If you have ever felt an earthquake, you were feeling the slipping and sliding of such plates.

Two of Earth's plates meet in California at the San Andreas Fault. A fault is the crack in the ground where plates meet.

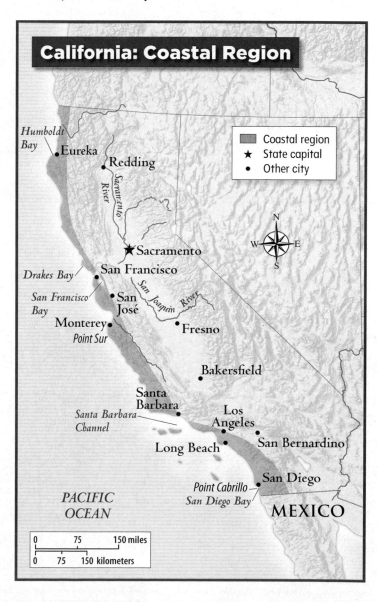

California: Coastal Region

- Coastal region
- ★ State capital
- • Other city

Humboldt Bay
Eureka
Redding
Sacramento River
Sacramento
San Francisco
Drakes Bay
San Francisco Bay
San José
San Joaquin River
Monterey
Point Sur
Fresno
Bakersfield
Santa Barbara
Santa Barbara Channel
Los Angeles
San Bernardino
Long Beach
San Diego
Point Cabrillo
San Diego Bay
PACIFIC OCEAN
MEXICO

0   75   150 miles
0   75   150 kilometers

Building for EARTHQUAKES

Designing safe buildings in earthquake-prone California is a challenge.

In California, earthquakes happen all the time. Even small earthquakes can knock down buildings. It is possible, though, to make cities safer. New ways of building can make the difference.

Earthquakes don't hit buildings head on. Instead they make buildings sway. Buildings that can sway back and forth just a little bit do best in earthquakes.

▼ **Even a small earthquake can destroy a big building.**

Joseph Sohm/Visions of America/Corbis

Renaud Visage/Alamy

Steel balls allow support columns to move in an earthquake.

An Earthquake-Proof Airport

The San Francisco International Airport was built to handle earthquakes. Here's how it works. There are 267 columns supporting the huge airport. Each column rides on a five-foot-wide steel ball. Each ball sits in a bowl-shaped base. Each bowl-shaped base is connected to the ground.

When the ground shakes, the balls roll around in their bases. The columns move a little bit. The building, though, doesn't fall down. When the earthquake is over, the balls roll back to the middle of their bases. The building goes back to normal.

Skyscrapers That Shake

If a huge skyscraper collapsed during an earthquake, it could kill hundreds of people. Luckily, skyscrapers are flexible. In an earthquake some are too flexible. They move like ocean waves. The people inside are hurt even if the building doesn't fall. One way to make skyscrapers safer is to make them stiffer so they move all in one piece. That way, the people inside don't get hurt.

There are other ideas to build safer skyscrapers. The TransAmerica Pyramid in San Francisco has a wide base but gets narrower as it goes up. Diagonal trusses at the base support the building. That way, no matter where an earthquake comes from, the building is supported.

▼ **Older structures can be made more earthquake-proof.**

Lacy Atkins/AP Photo

Fixing the Old Cities

There are many buildings in California that are not earthquake-proof. Houses and other buildings can be fixed, though, so that they don't collapse during an earthquake. Houses can be bolted to their foundations. Flexible gas pipes can be used so they don't break and cause fires. There's no way to stop an earthquake, but there are good ways to build safer cities. —*Lisa Jo Rudy*

AM Corporation/Alamy

Compare/Contrast Writing Frame

Use the Writing Frame below to orally summarize "Land Meets Water."

The coast of California has mountains. In Northern

California, some of the mountains _____.

The coast is often rocky and _____.

However, in Southern California the costal plain is _____

_____.

Unlike some parts of the northern coast, _____

_____.

California's northern and southern coasts have large cities.

Like San Diego and Los Angeles, the Bay Area _____

_____.

However, San Diego and Los Angeles are two of _____

_____.

Even though they differ in climate and geography, the northern and southern coasts are **both** exciting places to live or visit.

• • • • • • • • • • • • • • • • •

Use the frame to write the summary on another sheet of paper. Be sure to include the **bold** signal words. Keep this as a model of this Text Structure.

Critical Thinking

1 Earth's surface is made of huge _____.

    A. plates

    B. coasts

    C. mountains

2 Find the sentence in "Land Meets Water" that tells how long California's coastline is.

3 Locate the paragraph in "Building for Earthquakes" that explains how the San Francisco International Airport is built for earthquakes.

4 Review the map on page 109. How can a coastal map help your learn about California? Discuss your answer with a partner.

Special purpose maps show one feature of an area.

Digital Learning

For a list of links and activities that relate to this History/Social Science standard, visit the California Treasures Web site at www.macmillanmh.com to access the Content Readers resources. Have children view the video "The Golden State–Our Home."

CALIFORNIA'S FIRST PEOPLE

By the time the first Europeans sailed to North and South America, there were already millions of people living here. A large number of Native Americans, more than 300,000, lived in California.

Over time California's early people developed a great diversity, or range of differences, in the way they did things. This diversity came about as people learned to live with the resources of different climates. Wherever they settled, people used the natural resources around them to make their clothes, tools, and homes.

Groups who lived near the ocean developed special tools for catching and drying fish. Those who lived in valleys full of oak trees found ways to turn acorns into flour.

Over time, California's Native American peoples created at least 100 different cultures, or ways of life. They also developed 100 languages. Each group had its own crafts, customs, belief, and traditions.

Geographers divide the 100 groups into six main regions called **culture areas**. That means that all the groups living in each area have cultures that are alike in some important ways.

The cultural areas are Northwestern, Northeastern, Central, Great Basin, Southern, and Colorado River.

No one knows for certain how often people traveled beyond their local areas. We do know that they traded with one another. We also know that most of the Native Americans in California spoke at least two languages.

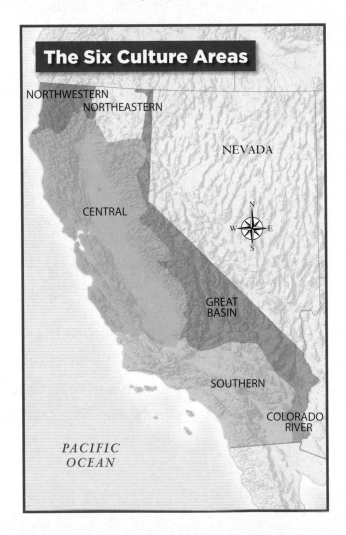

The Six Culture Areas

NORTHWESTERN
NORTHEASTERN
NEVADA
CENTRAL
GREAT BASIN
SOUTHERN
COLORADO RIVER
PACIFIC OCEAN

The Yokuts and numerous other peoples lived in the Central culture area. This was the largest of the six culture areas in California.

The Yokuts territory, in the San Joaquin Valley and the foothills of the Sierra Nevada, had many natural resources. The most important of these were the towering oak trees that filled the valley and the foothills. Their branches produced tons of acorns every fall.

If you were a Yokuts girl, you would have helped shake the acorns from the branches and gather the nuts. Then, with your mother, you would have packed the nuts away in a storage house, or **granary**.

Yokuts men spent much of their time hunting. In the fall, however, they took part in the acorn harvest. They would shake the branches to loosen the nuts for the women and children to pick up.

▼ A Yokuts woman pounds acorn to flour.

Yokuts communities burned parts of their land each year. The fires made ash, which kept the soil fertile. The fires also cleared away brush, leaving more land for wild game such as deer and antelope. This was just one of the many ways that Native Americans practiced **land management**, or care of the land.

In contrast the Northern Paiute lived in the Great Basin culture area. This area included the Sierra Nevada and Death Valley. The Northern Paiute, lived in a long strip of territory along what is now California's eastern boarder, next to Nevada.

In these areas, there were no oak trees to supply acorns or green valleys for good hunting. Even so, the Northern Paiute and other groups in the region were able to find sources of food.

These food sources, however, were not to be found in one place or all at one time. Their availability depended on the time of year. So, people had to stay on the move. They found fish and water birds in the shallow lakes created by water from the mountains in the early summer. Later in the year, they would climb the foothills of the Sierra Nevada, where they could hunt mountain sheep. Along the way, they would find places to catch hares.

The economy of the Northern Paiute was based on skillful hunting and gathering. To add to their resources, they traded with other groups for foods such as dried fish.

Salmon Run

Teenagers take action to save part of their heritage.

▲ **Kayla and Erika**

When they were 14, Kayla Carpenter and Erika Chase saw 64,000 salmon die. The fish died in the Klamath River in California. Kayla and Erika knew the river well. Friends since fourth grade, they had grown up fishing there. Kayla and Erika are Yurok and Hupa Indians. Salmon have sustained their communities for thousands of years.

Kayla and Erika describe the way their community felt about the death of the salmon this way: "Young and old cried in sadness and despair. We fear that with a few more years like this, our generation will see wild salmon become extinct in our rivers."

Making a Difference

"As Indian people and as young people, our future depends on the defense of our natural resources. We can all make a difference. All it takes is the spirit to act."
—Kayla Carpenter and Erika Chase

Water for farming or fish?

For more than 40 years, upstream dams have slowed water flow in the Klamath River. Dams make it possible to split up the river water. Much of the water goes to strawberry and cotton fields in the desert. Only a small amount is left for fish. It's not nearly enough.

Dams like this one on the Klamath River threaten the salmon.

▲ **The Salmon Run Relay**

The First Salmon Run Relay

In 2003, a year after the salmon died, Kayla and Erika organized the Salmon Run Relay. They wanted to educate and unite their communities, encourage local political involvement, and inspire exercise and healthier eating.

Volunteer runners carried a wooden fish 41 miles. The wooden fish symbolized salmon that swim in the river. The salmon come up the river to lay eggs. When the eggs hatch, the young fish swim to the ocean. The runners started at the mouth of the Klamath River and followed the route of the wild salmon. "The runners took on the salmon's struggle to call the world's attention," Erika says. It worked. The Salmon Run Relay is now an annual event.

The Award

In 2005, Kayla and Erika received the Earth Island Institute's Brower Youth Award. This is the highest environmental award for young people in the United States. —*Susan Moger*

The Hupa, Yurok, and Karuk Indians

These northern California Indians have lived along the Klamath and Trinity Rivers for thousands of years. Salmon have always been important in their cultures. Salmon were caught in the spring and fall as they returned to the rivers to spawn. Ceremonies were held to conserve this natural bounty.

The Yurok, Hupa, and Karuk traditions are alive and well. The Salmon Run Relay includes a salmon ceremony based on the ancient rituals of these Northern California Indians.

Problem/Solution Writing Frame

Use the Writing Frame below to orally summarize "Salmon Run."

Kayla Carpenter and Erika Chase were faced with a **problem**.

In the Klamath River _____

_____.

For the Yurok and Hupa Indians **this was a problem because**

_____

_____.

The problem occurred because _____

_____.

Only a small amount of water is left downriver for fish. Kayla and

Erika helped **solve this problem by** _____

_____

to raise awareness. It worked!

Use the frame to write the summary on another sheet of paper. Be sure to include the **bold** signal words. Keep this as a model of this Text Structure.

Critical Thinking

1 Which area is not one of the culture areas?

    A. Southwestern

    B. Northeastern

    C. Great Basin

2 Find the sentence in "California's First People" that explains land management.

3 Locate the section in "Salmon Run" that describes the route the runners follow.

4 Review the photograph on page 116 of one of the dams on the Klamath River. Discuss with a partner if the dams are helpful or harmful.

Photographs and captions give visual examples that help explain what the text states.

Digital Learning

For a list of links and activities that relate to this History/Social Science standard, visit the California Treasures Web site at www.macmillanmh.com to access the Content Readers resources. Have children view A Day in the Life "A Young Native American's Life in California."

EXPLORATIONS OF CABRILLO

In 1542 the **viceroy**, or ruler, of New Spain gave Juan Rodriguez Cabrillo (kah•BREE•yoh) the job of exploring the coast of California. New Spain was the Spanish colony in North America made up of all or parts of the land now called Mexico, Central America, and the United States.

Cabrillo was a conquistador and a sea captain. **Conquistadors** (kon•KEES•tuh•dorz) is the Spanish word for soldiers who seized land by force.

On June 27, 1542, Cabrillo and his crew set sail with two small ships, the *San Salvador* and the *Victoria*. On September 28, 1542, the ships sailed into a bay. Cabrillo named the bay San Miguel. Later explorers would rename the bay San Diego.

Cabrillo described the area as "closed and very good." They explored the land and met the local Kumeyaay people. Cabrillo and his men spent six days there before continuing north.

After leaving San Diego, Cabrillo and his crew sailed to what is today known as Santa Catalina Island.

Cabrillo traveled farther north along the coast. On the islands of San Miguel, Santa Cruz, and Santa Rosa outside the Santa Barbara Channel he and his crew found large populations of Native Americans.

The **expedition**, journey of exploration, soon passed into the Santa Barbara Channel. On one of the islands in the channel, Cabrillo and his men saw a Native American

Cabrillo reached the Channel Islands in 1542.

The Beginning of New Spain

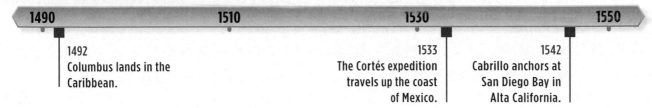

1490	1510	1530	1550

1492
Columbus lands in the Caribbean.

1533
The Cortés expedition travels up the coast of Mexico.

1542
Cabrillo anchors at San Diego Bay in Alta California.

town with large adobe houses. Some residents rowed out in canoes to greet them.

Cabrillo claimed the land he found for New Spain. He called it "Alta California," or upper California. Cabrillo named the town he found "Pueblo de las Canoas", the Town of the Canoes.

The people Cabrillo met were the Chumash. They told Cabrillo that if he traveled farther north, he would find a large river flowing into the sea. The explorers set sail, but met high winds and rough seas. They turned back after about one month to wait for better weather.

Cabrillo's dealings with Native Americans had been friendly to this point. However, the Chumash on the Channel Islands were eager for the explorers to leave their land. On December 24, 1542, men from Cabrillo's ships were attacked. While trying to rescue them, Cabrillo broke his arm. He would die from the injury.

Before dying, Cabrillo asked Bartolomé Ferrelo, his chief pilot, to take charge of the expedition. Ferrelo ordered the men to bury their leader on the island where he died. Today that island is called San Miguel Island.

Bad weather forced Ferrelo to wait until late February 1543 to leave the Channel Islands and head north. Soon after, the ships ran into another storm and were damaged. Ferrelo decided to end the expedition. Historians think he had reached the boarder of present day Oregon.

The expeditions by Cabrillo and Ferrelo discovered many harbors of Baja and Alta California. From the voyage's journals, historians have identified 70 locations. The crew explored lands that no Europeans had seen before.

This statue of Cabrillo stands in San Diego.

CALIFORNIA AND CATTLE

Cattle ranching became big business for Catholic missions in the days when Spain controlled California.

The year was 1769. The place was Baja California—the southern part of Spain's colony north of Mexico. Spain was in charge, but Russians were starting to move south from Alaska. The king of Spain was worried. How could he hold California and build his empire?

The king's solution to this question was a man, Father Junipero Serra. Serra was a Catholic priest. He had worked in Mexico for many years. Serra landed his boats in San Diego, California. He brought along several hundred head of cattle.

Building Spanish Missions

The first part of Serra's job was to build missions. Missions were buildings in which priests lived and held religious services. Around the mission buildings were farms and ranches that produced food for the people who lived in the mission.

Bringing Indians to the Missions

The second part of Serra's job was to convince American Indians to come to the missions. If the American Indians became Christians, they would support the Spanish. The Russians would be outnumbered.

▼ **Mission San Carlos Borromeo del Rio Carmelo, in Carmel, California, as it looks today.**

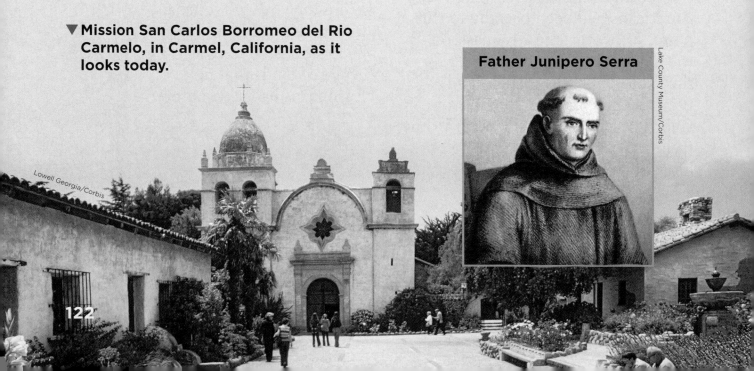

Lowell Georgia/Corbis

Father Junipero Serra

Lake County Museum/Corbis

Lake County Museum/Corbis

Corbis

◀ **Mission Santa Clara de Asis, in Santa Clara**

▲ **Mission Indians making rope and baskets**

Serra built nine missions up and down the California coast. He and other priests worked to bring in Indians. Sometimes the Indians came on their own. Sometimes the Indians were tricked or forced into coming to the missions. At the missions, Indians learned about Christianity and the Spanish language. They also learned about ranching and cattle.

Cattle Ranching Catches On

California weather was perfect for raising cattle. In 1774 there were about 350 head of longhorn cattle in California. By 1834 there were 396,000!

When California became part of the United States in 1848, the Spanish missions stopped ranching.

The longhorn cattle, though, became a part of California life. Cow skins (leather) were worth a lot of money. Californians traded with ships' captains for almost everything they needed.

The End of an Era

In 1864 there was a terrible drought. Many of the cattle died. Ranchers had to find other ways to make money. A few years later ranchers bought more cattle, and their ranches were back in business. Even so, the golden age of ranching was over. —*Lisa Jo Rudy*

Longhorn cattle were an important part of California's economy. ▶

DLILLC/Corbis

Sequence Writing Frame

Use the Writing Frame below to orally summarize "Explorations of Cabrillo."

In June of 1542, _____

_____ .

On September 28, 1542, _____

_____ . Cabrillo named the bay San Miguel.

Next they explored _____

_____ .

After leaving San Miguel, _____

_____ .

On December 24, 1542, _____

_____ . While trying to rescue them,

Cabrillo broke his arm. **Later** _____

_____ .

Use the frame to write the summary on another sheet of paper.
Be sure to include the **bold** signal words. Keep this as a model
of this Text Structure.

Critical Thinking

1 The Spanish word for soldiers who seized land by force is _____ .

    A. viceroy

    B. conquistadors

    C. expedition

2 Find the sentence in "California and Cattle" that explains what missions were.

3 Locate the section in "California and Cattle" that describes the importance of Native Americans to the missions.

4 Review the time line on page 121. Point to where you would place Ferrelo. Share with a partner.

> Time lines show historical events in the order in which they occurred.

Digital Learning

For a list of links and activities that relate to this History/Social Science standard, visit the California Treasures Web site at www.macmillanmh.com to access the Content Readers resources. Have children view the video "Early California History."

THE MEXICAN WAR FOR INDEPENDENCE

For 300 years Spain sent officials across the Atlantic Ocean to rule New Spain. Mexican colonist grew tired of being ruled by faraway Spain. They learned how the United States had won its freedom from Great Britain. They wanted their freedom too. In 1810 they went to war with Spain to win independence.

The Mexican War for Independence lasted 11 years. When it finally ended in 1821, Mexico was an independent country, free of Spanish rule.

The fighting took place in Mexico, far from California. Many people in California did not find out that Mexico had won the war until 1822. When they heard the news, the Californios, as the Mexican people in California called themselves, raised their new flag.

Under Mexico's new government, life changed for the people of California. One big change was that the government decided to close the Spanish settlements, called missions, where priests taught Native Americans the Christian religion.

The Mexican government made this decision for several reasons. The missions were on valuable land. The Californios wanted this land for ranches and farms. Also, many Mexicans believed that Native Americans were not being treated fairly at the missions. Some Native Americans led revolts against the missions. The new government's leaders said that all people were equal.

In 1834, California's new governor, José Figueroa, ordered that missions closed. He hoped that closing them would stop the revolts. Figueroa also ordered half the mission lands given to the Native Americans who had lived and worked there.

Many Californios supported Governor Figueroa's plan because they hoped to win some of the mission lands for themselves. The Mexican government began to give out most of the mission lands in larger pieces, known as **land grants**.

Any Mexican citizen could apply for a land grant. However, Californio land owners and soldiers from the presidios received most of the first land grants. Native Americans received few.

The Californios turned their new land into more than 500 ranchos. A rancho was a ranch where cattle, horses, and other animals were raised. Mariano Guadalupe Vallejo became one of the richest **rancheros**, or ranch owners. He became an army commander and went into politics. As a politician, Vallejo would play an important role in California.

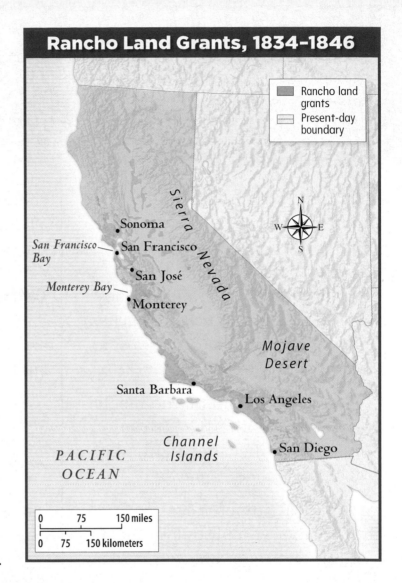

Rancho Land Grants, 1834–1846

Rancho land grants
Present-day boundary

Sonoma
San Francisco Bay
San Francisco
San José
Monterey Bay
Monterey
Sierra Nevada
Mojave Desert
Santa Barbara
Los Angeles
Channel Islands
San Diego
PACIFIC OCEAN

0   75   150 miles
0   75   150 kilometers

Ranchos of California

Cattle-ranching was big business in California in the 1800s.

▲ "San Juan Capistrano" brand

After Mexico won independence from Spain in 1821, life in California changed. The Catholic missions lost land and power. Enormous tracts of land were granted to wealthy families. They were turned into *ranchos* (ranches) and were devoted to cattle-raising. The owners were called *rancheros*.

Most of the work on the ranchos was done by California Indians. Some Indians became highly skilled cowhands, called *vaqueros*.

A typical rancho might have from 20 to several hundred Indian workers. The workers weren't paid wages. They were given food, shelter, and clothing instead. Violence was often used to keep the workers in line.

Cattle Economy

Ranchos had huge herds of cattle and many acres of prime grazing land. There were no fences, so cattle from different ranchos would get mixed together. To help the rancheros figure out which cattle belonged to whom, the cattle were branded—a mark identifying the owner was burned into the cow's hide.

▼ **Vaqueros at work**

The Granger Collection

Eventually, the cattle were rounded up, sorted by owner, and then killed. The hides were valuable. They were used to make leather saddles, shoes, and other products. Fat from the cattle was boiled down into tallow. Tallow was used to make soap and candles.

California was still part of Mexico. Traders from the United States and other countries traded factory-made goods for the hides and tallow.

Rancho Life

With work done by others, rich land owners enjoyed a comfortable life on the ranchos. It was a life dedicated to family and tradition —and beef. They ate beef for breakfast, lunch, and dinner. Amusements included grizzly bear hunts, bull and bear fighting, and weddings! —*Susan Moger*

▲ **A 1906 photograph of a rancho in Inyo County, California**

Prudencia Higuera—Trading for Toothbrushes

In 1840 Prudencia Higuera, a member of a ranchero family, described how her family traded with a ship from the United States.

My brothers, with the [workers], drove [the cattle] to the beach, killed them there, and salted the hides. They [melted] the tallow in some iron kettles. The captain [of the U.S. ship] soon came to our landing with a small boat and two sailors.

The captain looked over the hides and then asked my father to get into the boat and go to the vessel. [My father] came back the next day, bringing four boat-loads of cloth, axes, shoes, fish-lines, and many new things. There were two grindstones and some cheap jewelry. My brother traded for a gun and four toothbrushes. [They were] the first ones I had ever seen.

Cause/Effect Writing Frame

Use the Writing Frame below to orally summarize "Ranchos of California."

In 1821 Mexico won independence from Spain. One **effect** this had

on California was that the Catholic missions _____

_____ .

Because some people received _____

this caused the rise of an elite group of _____ .

Because the track of lands granted to wealthy families, were so large,

most of the work _____ .

This explains why some Indians _____
called vaqueros.

The workers weren't paid wages, but they _____

_____ instead.

With work done by others, rich landowners enjoyed a comfortable
life. **The result was that** rancheros were able to dedicate

_____ .

Use the frame to write the summary on another sheet of paper.
Be sure to include the **bold** signal words. Keep this as a model of
this Text Structure.

Critical Thinking

1. An area of free land the Mexican government gave to Mexicans who settled in California was called a _____.

   A. rancho

   B. land grant

   C. farm

2. Point to the sentence in "Ranchos of California" that explains the word *branded*.

3. Locate the section in "The Mexican War for Independence" that explains who could apply for a land grant.

4. Review the map on page 127 with a partner. Discuss the location of rancho land grants. Are more located in the east, west, north, or south?

   A key or legend helps you interpret the colors or special symbols on a map.

Digital Learning

For a list of links and activities that relate to this History/Social Science standard, visit the California Treasures Web site at www.macmillanmh.com to access the Content Readers resources. Have children view A Day in the Life "A Young Person's Life in the 1840s."

THE FUR TRADE

In the early 1800s Russian fur hunters sailed down the coast of California, which was still a part of Mexico, from Alaska. In 1812 they built a settlement called Fort Ross about 50 miles north of San Francisco.

Fort Ross was the Russians' base for hunting sea otters and seals, which were valuable for their **pelts**. A pelt is the fur-covered hide of an animal.

At the time, fur coats and hats were popular because they were soft, warm, and waterproof.

The Russians weren't the only people interested in fur. American **trappers** soon headed for California in search of beaver pelts. A trapper is someone who catches animals for their fur.

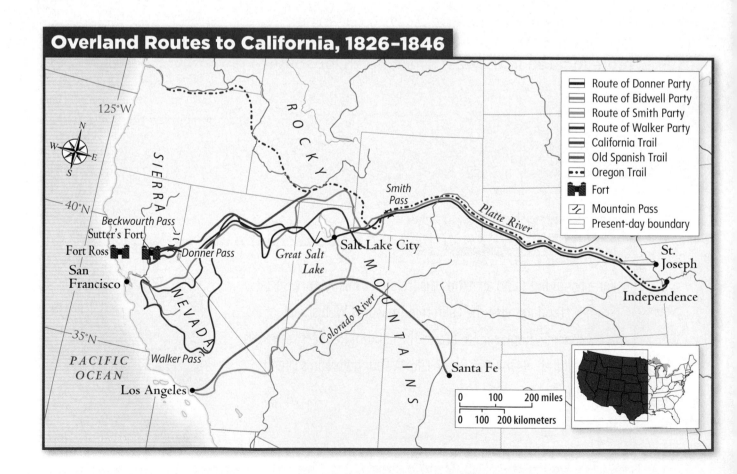

Overland Routes to California, 1826–1846

Many pioneer families walked beside their covered wagons.

Jebediah Strong Smith believed there were a lot of beavers in California. In 1826 he led a group of 15 trappers there. They were the first people from the United States to journey to California over land.

The group left on August 16, 1826, from what is now Utah. They traveled southwest through mountains and deserts.

In early October the group reached the Colorado River near California. With the help of Native American guides, they made it across the Mojave Desert. On November 27, Smith and the other trappers arrived at Mission San Gabriel. There they heard that the San Joaquin Valley was filled with

beavers. However, the Mexican governor thought Smith was an American spy and ordered him to leave California.

In 1839 a man named Johann Sutter arrived in California. He would play an important part in California's history. Sutter was a businessman from Switzerland. After landing in Monterey in 1839, he received a land grant in the Sacramento Valley. He built a large settlement there, including a fort.

New settlers to California often stopped at Sutter's Fort. The settlers came mostly from Eastern states. They were called **pioneers**.

Sutter's Fort

John Sutter struck it rich in California–until the Gold Rush came along.

When John Sutter set out from his home in Switzerland in the 1834, his businesses were failing. He headed to the United States. In 1838, he joined a trapping party that was headed for the Pacific Coast. From Vancouver, he sailed to Hawaii.

In Hawaii, Sutter pretended to be a successful captain in the Swiss Guards. He persuaded important Hawaiians to lend him money. Then he sailed off to California with a group of nine Hawaiians.

Building New Switzerland

In 1839, California was still part of Mexico. Sutter asked the Mexican government for land. The government agreed. Sutter and his Hawaiian friends headed up the Sacramento River. They landed near what is now the town of Sacramento.

Sutter soon met a large group of American Indians. He offered the Indians work.

▲ **John Sutter**

Soon Sutter and the Indians were friends. Together they turned Sutter's 48,827 acres of land into New Helvetia (meaning "New Switzerland").

In 1840, Sutter started building a fort. The fort protected a growing community that included Mexicans, Hawaiians, and Indians. New Helvetia had large herds of cattle and horses. Hunters from the community gathered fur pelts and elk hides. Sutter built a flour mill, bakery, blacksmith shop, and carpenter shop.

Sutter's Fort was completed in 1844. It grew in importance as more settlers arrived. It gained a reputation for hospitality.

Gold! The End of Sutter's Fort

Then came the beginning of the end. In 1847, Sutter started building a sawmill for a man named James Marshall. He was almost finished in 1848 when Marshall discovered gold in the water.

By 1849 thousands of people were rushing to California to prospect for gold. The Gold Rush hurt Sutter. His workmen quit to look for gold. Gold prospectors rushed through the area, stealing Sutter's land, crops, and animals. Sutter tried to sell goods to the miners, but he was cheated. Soon he was out of money. Leaving his land to his son, John Jr., Sutter moved away. Young John Sutter Jr. started creating the new town of Sacramento. But his father moved to Lititz, Pennsylvania, with his wife.

John Sutter Sr. died soon afterward. He had lost the empire he built. His work, however, lived on. —*Lisa Jo Rudy*

▼ **An 1855 painting of miners at Sutter's Mill**

The Bancroft Library

▼ **Sutter's Fort today**

Robert Holmes/Corbis

Sutter's Fort, shown in an illustration from 1849

The Bancroft Library

Compare/Contrast Writing Frame

Use the Writing Frame below to orally summarize "The Fur Trade."

Russian and American settlers were **similar** in many ways. They were

alike because _____ .

In addition, **they both** journeyed to _____

and _____ .

In some ways, however, _____ and _____

settlers were **different**. They were **different** because some Russian

fur hunters _____ .

However, some American settlers journeyed to California _____

_____ .

Another **difference** was that Russians were hunting _____ ,

while Americans were _____ .

So _____ and _____ settlers
were **alike** in some ways and **different** in others.

• • • • • • • • • • • • • • • • •

Use the frame to write the summary on another sheet of paper.
Be sure to include the **bold** signal words. Keep this as a model of
this Text Structure.

Critical Thinking

1. The first people to settle in a region are _____.

   A. pioneers

   B. trappers

   C. immigrants

2. Locate the sentence in "The Fur Trade" that defines what a pelt is.

3. Reread the paragraph in "Sutter's Fort" that explains the beginning of the end of Sutter's Fort.

4. Look at the photograph and illustrations on page 135. Discuss with a partner how they support the text.

> Photographs give visual examples that help explain what the text states.

Digital Learning

For a list of links and activities that relate to this History/Social Science standard, visit the California Treasures Web site at www.macmillanmh.com to access the Content Readers resources. Have children view the video "Becoming A State."

GOLD IS FOUND

On January 24, 1849, a crew of men was hard at work on a project for Johann Sutter. Sutter was a Swiss immigrant to Mexican California who founded Sutter's Fort. Standing knee-deep in the American River, they were clearing large stones from the riverbed. Suddenly, one of them let out a cry. He had spotted something shiny, "about the size of a pea." The minute he touched it, he said later, "It made my heart thump, for I was certain it was gold."

As the news of the discovery of gold spread around the world, people left everything behind and headed to California. This rapid movement of people in search of gold is known as the **Gold Rush**. Nearly 80,000 gold seekers from around the world came to California during 1849. They were called **forty-niners**.

By the spring of 1849 thousands of people were ready to leave for California. They could choose one of three different routes.

The first route was entirely by sea and went all the way around South America. The trip took four to eight months by cargo ship. Some travelers shortened this time by paying more to travel by **clipper ship**. Clipper ships were sleek and slim, with many more sails than ordinary ships.

Life on board any ship was hard. The ships were usually crowded. The food was often stale or moldy. There was little fresh water to drink. However, the worst part of the journey was getting around Cape Horn and the tip of South America. Terrible storms sank many ships off Cape Horn.

◀ Sutter's Mill, where gold was first found in California.

138

The second route was also by sea, but included a "shortcut." Travelers went by ship to Panama, in Central America. There, they crossed the Isthmus of Panama. An isthmus (IS•muhs) is a narrow strip of land. People crossed the Isthmus on foot, by mule, and in small boats. It was a difficult journey through swamps and jungles.

Once they had crossed the Isthmus, travelers had to wait for another ship on Panama's Pacific Coast. This ship took them north to San Francisco.

The third route was overland by wagon train. The largest number of travelers chose this route. It was not only the cheapest way to travel, but it allowed them to bring horses, cattle, supplies and household goods.

When Bayard Taylor, a forty-niner from New York arrived in San Francisco, he saw

"Hundreds of tents and houses . . . scattered all over the [hills] . . . buildings of all kinds, begun or half-finished . . . covered with all kinds of signs in all languages. . . . Goods were piled in the open air. . . . The streets were full of people. . . . One knows not whether he is awake or in some wonderful dream."

There were so many people that there were not enough hotels or houses for all of them. Stores opened up everywhere. Some stores were built in the ships that sailors had left in the harbor.

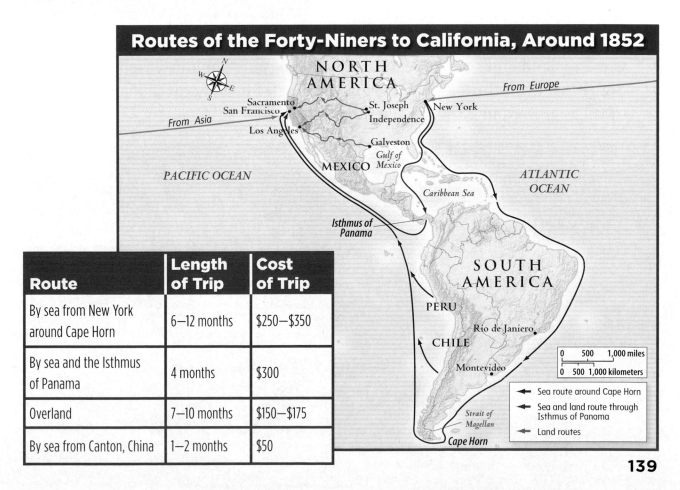

Routes of the Forty-Niners to California, Around 1852

Route	Length of Trip	Cost of Trip
By sea from New York around Cape Horn	6–12 months	$250–$350
By sea and the Isthmus of Panama	4 months	$300
Overland	7–10 months	$150–$175
By sea from Canton, China	1–2 months	$50

GOLD RUSH GLORY

The California Gold Rush inspired a lot of people to venture west. Here are the stories of two men who made names for themselves.

On January 24, 1848, James Marshall discovered gold at Sutter's Mill. Sutter's Mill was a sawmill owned by John Sutter in north central California. That discovery started the famous California Gold Rush.

In the end, more than 300,000 people traveled to California in search of gold. They were men and women of all races and all ages. They came by land and sea. Some gold seekers became fabulously rich. Some lost everything. They were called forty-niners because many of them arrived in 1849. —*Lisa Jo Rudy*

Corbis

▲ **Sutter's Mill in 1852**

▼ **Gold mining in California during the Gold Rush**

Bettmann/Corbis

Bettmann/Corbis

James Beckwourth

James Beckwourth was born in Virginia in 1798. His mother was a slave. Beckwourth was one of the few black men to take part in the Gold Rush, and the only one to record his story.

Early in life, Beckwourth went to live with the Crow and Blackfoot Indians. Then he made his way to California for the Gold Rush. One day, Beckwourth noticed what looked like a gap through the Sierra Nevada. If he had discovered a safe and easy way to cross the Sierras, he could open up a new trade route.

The next spring, Beckwourth led a party to explore the gap. They made it to the eastern slope of the Sierras!

The Beckwourth Pass was opened in 1851, and Beckwourth himself led the first party through. The pass still carries Beckwourth's name.

Mary Evans Picture Library/The Image Works

John Charles Fremont

John Charles Fremont was born in Georgia in 1813. He left home early, and went into the army. Then, in 1841, Fremont married Jessie Benton. Jessie was part of an important family. Her father was a senator.

In 1842, Fremont led two expeditions to the West. He discovered new routes to Oregon. He earned the name the Great Pathfinder.

Fremont then became an important soldier. In 1850, he became a senator from the brand-new state of California. In 1856, John Fremont ran for president of the United States, but lost. After the Civil War, Fremont's life went downhill. Though he became governor of Arizona, he didn't do a very good job. His money was disappearing, too. When he died, he had no money left. But he had changed the American West forever.

Fremont plants a U.S. flag on the Colorado Rockies, 1842. ▶

Northwind Picture Archives

141

Sequence Writing Frame

Use the Writing Frame below to orally summarize "Gold Rush Glory."

The California Gold Rush inspired a lot of people to venture west. One of them was James Beckwourth.

James Beckwourth's life **began** _____

_____ .

His mother _____ .

Early in life _____ .

Then _____
for the Gold Rush.

One day while walking through northern California, Beckwourth

_____ .

The next spring, _____ .

The gap led them to _____ .

In 1851 _____ .

Today, the pass still carries Beckwourth's name.

Use the frame to write the summary on another sheet of paper. Be sure to include the **bold** signal words. Keep this as a model of this Text Structure.

Critical Thinking

1 Sleek, fast sailing ships were known as _____ .

    A. clipper ships

    B. cargo ships

    C. forty-niner ships

2 Point to the sentence in "Gold Is Found" that tells why people were called forty-niners.

3 Find the paragraph in "Gold Rush Glory" that explains how John Charles Fremont received the nickname the Great Pathfinder.

4 Study the chart on page 139. With a partner, explain which route you would take to California.

Charts organize information and make it easy to read and remember.

Digital Learning

For a list of links and activities that relate to this History/Social Science standard, visit the California Treasures Web site at www.macmillanmh.com to access the Content Readers resources. Have children view the Biography "James Beckwourth."

THE ROAD TO STATEHOOD

After the Mexican War ended in 1848, California was a part of the United States, but it was not a state. Military governors were chosen by the United States government in Washington, D.C. The people of California could not vote or choose their leaders. The old Mexican laws were still used, and there was no court system.

This system had worked as long as California remained a rancho economy. Once gold was discovered, however, everything changed.

The Gold Rush brought thousands of people from all over the world. Mining camps and towns were forming. The new arrivals in California wanted to make their own laws. Each mining area was making and enforcing its own rules. These different rules were confusing and often unfair.

General Bennett F. Riley, the last military governor, knew that he must act. Otherwise he could have trouble on his hands. He called for Californians to choose **delegates**, or people who would represent them.

▲ General Bennett F. Riley, last military governor of California.

The delegates would come to a **convention**, or meeting, at Colton Hall in Monterey. This meeting would be the first step in writing a **constitution**. A constitution is a plan of government. The constitution would decide the size of California and the rights of its citizens.

The delegates made some important decisions. They had to choose whether to ask the U.S. Congress to make California a state or a territory. They decided to ask for statehood. Further, they decided that California would be a free state. This meant that California would not allow slavery. The delegates also decided that the Sierra Nevada and the Colorado River would be the eastern boundaries of California.

On September 9, 1850, California became the 31st state in the nation. That date is now celebrated each year as Admission Day.

The new state government chose the city of San Jose as its capital, or government center. However, the capital would move to three other cities before Sacramento became the permanent capital in 1954.

There were important differences between the new state government and those under the Spanish and Mexican periods. Under Spanish and Mexican rule, the governor of California was appointed. The governor of the state of California was elected.

Room in Colton Hall, Monterey, where delegates met to discuss California's constitution.

145

Biddy Mason

This remarkable woman went from slave in Mississippi to businesswoman in California.

▲ **Bridget (Biddy) Mason**

Bridget "Biddy" Mason was born August 15, 1818, in Mississippi. She was born a slave on a plantation owned by Robert and Rebecca Smith. Mason had three daughters, Ellen, Ann, and Harriet.

In 1847, Robert Smith joined the Mormon Church. He decided to move his family across the United States to the Utah Territory. It was a 2,000-mile trip. Biddy Mason and her daughters went along. It was Mason's job to herd the cattle. She was also in charge of cooking and, of course, she took care of her own children.

In 1851, Smith moved again. This time, he headed for San Bernardino, California. Brigham Young, the founder of the Mormon Church, was starting a community there.

What Smith might not have known was that California was a free state. Slavery was against the law.

In California, Mason learned about the law against slavery and went to the court. She explained that she was being kept as a slave, against state law. In 1856, the California courts made Mason a free woman.

Slaves picking cotton on a plantation in the South, early 1800s ▼

Corbis

Golden State Mutual Insurance Records, Collection 1434
box 41 Biddy Mason House, 1844

Mason left Smith's household and moved to Los Angeles with her daughters. There she became a nurse and midwife (a person who helps women to give birth). Mason worked hard and saved her money.

Ten years after gaining her freedom, she had enough money to buy land. She was one of the first black women to buy property in Los Angeles.

In 1884, Mason sold part of her land for a good profit. She put up a building on the rest of the land and rented out space to businesses. Then she continued to make money in real estate. By the time she died, Mason had made a fortune! Her grandson, Robert Curry Owens, was a real estate developer and politician. He became one of the richest men in Los Angeles.

▲ **Biddy Mason's home, photographed in the 1870s**

Mason also became famous for her generosity. She gave money to charities and gave food and shelter to people in need. She was so well loved that a special memorial was built in her honor. It was unveiled in 1989. —*Lisa Jo Rudy*

▼ **Memorial wall in Los Angeles honoring Biddy Mason**

Peter Bennett/CaliforniaStockPhoto

Problem/Solution Writing Frame

Use the Writing Frame below to orally summarize "The Road to Statehood."

In 1848, California was a part of the United States, but it was not

a state. **This was a problem because** _____

_____.

This problem happened because before the Mexican War,

California _____.

After the war, old Mexican laws _____.

To solve this problem, General Riley called for Californians to _____

_____.

The delegates had to make important decisions. **The result** was

that they asked the U. S. Congress _____

_____.

On September 9, 1850, California became the 31st state in
the nation.

Use the frame to write the summary on another sheet of paper.
Be sure to include the **bold** signal words. Keep this as a model of
this Text Structure.

Critical Thinking

1 A _____ is a plan of government.

   A. delegate

   B. convention

   C. constitution

2 Find the sentence in "Biddy Mason" that explains what a midwife is.

3 Point to the place in "The Road to Statehood" that mentions an important difference between the new state government of California and those under Spanish and Mexican periods.

4 Select your favorite photo from "Biddy Mason." Orally create a new caption for it.

> Captions may give more information about the photograph or the article.

Digital Learning

For a list of links and activities that relate to this History/Social Science standard, visit the California Treasures Web site at www.macmillanmh.com to access the Content Readers resources. Have children view the video "Becoming a State."

THE PONY EXPRESS

In the 1850s, California's population was growing rapidly, but great distances separated the state from the eastern United States. It took months for news, mail, supplies, and people to reach the West Coast. California needed better **communication** with the rest of the country. Communication is the exchange of information between people.

To speed communication the U.S. government hired **stagecoach** companies to deliver the mail. A stagecoach was a carriage pulled by a team of horses. Stagecoaches stopped at stations along their routes to change horses. They provided faster **transportation** than wagon trains. Transportation is the movement of people and goods.

It took a stagecoach from the Overland Mail Service three weeks to travel the 2,800 miles from Missouri to San Francisco. Each coach carried about 170 pounds of letters and 140 pounds of newspapers.

On April 13, 1860, Billy Hamilton made the first delivery for the Pony Express. The Pony Express was the fastest mail service to California at the time. It was set up like a relay race.

Each rider passed a bag of mail to the rider waiting ahead of him. The riders traveled day and night. Each rider had a regular run, or route, separated by a number of stations. A rider set off from a station with a mail bag and galloped 10 to 15 miles to the next station. There the rider would quickly change to a fresh horse and ride on to the next station. After about eight stations, or 80 to 100 miles, a new rider took over. At the end of a run, a rider ate and slept at the station house until it was time to make the return trip.

As fast as it was, the Pony Express mail service only lasted 18 months. It was replaced by a new technology.

The new technology soon allowed Californians to communicate in seconds instead of weeks or day. The telegraph could send messages to distant places almost instantly by using electricity. The inventor and artist Samuel F. B. Morse developed the first telegraph in 1836. He also helped design the code that is known as Morse code. Morse code uses patterns of dots and dashes to stand for each letter of the alphabet. Morse code was used to send telegraph messages.

By 1861 telegraph lines stretched from coast to coast. The lines were strung from poles that ran along railroad tracks. Most of the lines belonged to the Western Union Telegraph Company.

A coast-to-coast telegraph system was completed on October 24, 1861. Soon after, the Pony Express went out of business. Technology replaced the horse in the communication race.

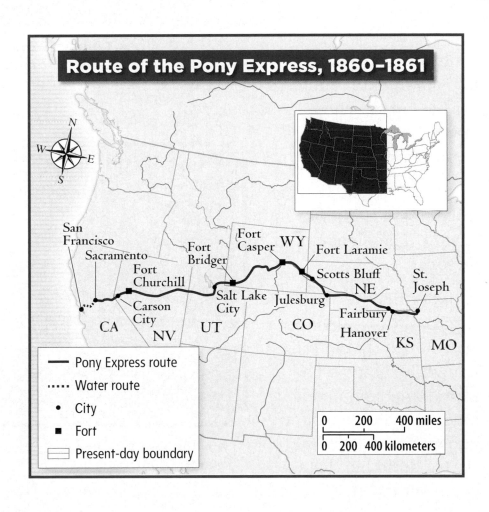

Route of the Pony Express, 1860–1861

151

A Chinese-American Marriage

In the late 1800s a remarkable California family was founded by a Chinese man and an American woman.

The Granger Collection

In 1871, Fong See left his village in China and headed for Sacramento, California. He was searching for his father, who had disappeared while helping to build the transcontinental railroad.

At about the same time, Letticie Pruett's family crossed America in a covered wagon. They made their home in Oregon.

Fong See didn't find his father, but he did find work. By the late 1890s, Fong See owned a clothing factory. Meanwhile, Letticie had run away from home and ended up in Sacramento. Letticie wound up in Chinatown and asked Fong See for a job. He hired her. Later, they decided to get married.

▲ **Chinese workers on the transcontinental railroad**

The Granger Collection

▲ **A Chinese butcher in California, around 1900**

In the 1890s it was against the law in California and many other states for Chinese and white people to marry. Chinese people could not own property or be citizens. They could not even immigrate to the United States.

In spite of these problems, a lawyer helped Fong See and Letticie draw up a marriage contract. They married and eventually moved from Sacramento to Los Angeles. They raised five children. They ran five antique stores. Fong See became the first Chinese person in the United States to own a car. He even sold props to the brand-new movie industry.

Even though Fong See and Letticie married and were successful, the laws did not change. All of their four sons chose to marry Caucasian women. They had to go to Mexico to marry.

The laws that made life difficult for Fong See, Letticie, and their children did not change for a long time. Similar laws made life terrible for African Americans and Native Americans. Finally, in 1965 mixed-race marriages became legal across the United States.

Today many people marry outside of their race or cultural background. People's families come from all over the world as well as right next door. —*Lisa Jo Rudy*

▲ **Discrimination against the Chinese was common.**

▲ **Author Lisa See is the great-granddaughter of Fong See and Letticie See.**

▲ **Diverse families are common today.**

153

Sequence Writing Frame

**Use the Writing Frame below to orally summarize
"A Chinese-American Marriage."**

In the late 1800s a remarkable California family was founded by a
Chinese man and an American woman.

In 1871 _____.

By the late 1890's Fong See _____

_____.

Meanwhile Letticie _____.

Fong See gave her a job _____.

Later _____.

In 1890 it was _____.

However, they married and moved to Los Angeles. Next, they _____

_____.

The laws that made life difficult for Fong See, Letticie, and their

children did not change for a long time. **Finally**, in 1965, _____

_____.

Use the frame to write the summary on another sheet of paper.
Be sure to include the **bold** signal words. Keep this as a model of
this Text Structure.

Critical Thinking

1 _____ is the movement of people and goods.

   A. Communication

   B. Stagecoach

   C. Transportation

2 Locate the name of the technology in "The Pony Express" that replaced the pony express.

3 Find the text in "A Chinese-American Marriage" that explains the laws against Chinese people in the 1890s.

4 Look at the map on page 151. Discuss the route of the Pony Express with a partner.

Labels identify cities, states, rivers, or other land features.

Digital Learning

For a list of links and activities that relate to this History/Social Science standard, visit the California Treasures Web site at www.macmillanmh.com to access the Content Readers resources. Have children view the video "A Growing State."

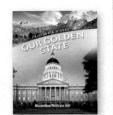

LAND OF OPPORTUNITY

At the end of the 1800s, many people came to California seeking a new life. Some came to escape harsh conditions back home. Others came looking for gold or jobs on railroads and farms. All were seeking a chance to build a better life for their families.

When large numbers of newcomers move to a place it is called **migration**. People who lived in other parts of the United States moved to California. Others came from all over the world. People who move to a new county are known as **immigrants**.

Immigrants came for many reasons. Some came to escape poverty or wars at home. Others were drawn by newspaper ads. In 1913 a farmer advertised for people to help with a harvest. His ad brought workers from 27 different countries.

The land, climate, and economic growth in California gave many immigrants the chance to earn a living by farming. Some newcomers were able to buy their own land. Others made a life for themselves in California's cities.

Immigrants from Russia, Poland, and Korea settled in such places as Los Angeles, San Francisco, and San Diego. They worked in factories, in restaurants, and on boats as fishermen.

Immigrants also started one of the most important companies in Hollywood. In the mid-1920s, two young immigrants—Samuel Goldwyn from Poland and Luis B. Mayer from Russia—created a film company. The company was called Metro-Goldwyn-Mayer (MGM) and it went on to become one of Hollywood's biggest film studios.

Many immigrants to California came through Angel Island.

Immigrants who came from the same country were drawn together by their common cultures. Members of some immigrant groups settled together in neighborhoods in large cities. Mexican immigrants created their own communities within cities. In these neighborhoods, called **barrios**, Spanish was spoken.

Immigrant communities also supported new arrivals from their homelands by forming **mutual aid societies**. These organizations helped new immigrants find housing and jobs. The Mexican mutual aid societies were called **mutualistas**.

Some immigrant groups founded their own towns. The city of Anaheim was founded by German immigrants in 1857. They worked together on farms and shared the profits.

Competition for jobs and difference in culture often led to feelings of dislike, or **prejudice**, against immigrants. Often people acted on these feelings by treating immigrants unfairly. This kind of unfair treatment is called discrimination. Many immigrant communities in California worked to defend their members from discrimination and prejudice.

Immigrant Communities in California, 1900–1930

- Armenian
- Chinese
- Danish
- German
- Italian Swiss
- Japanese
- Many immigrant groups

Asti · Yuba City · Sacramento · San Francisco · Yamato Colony · Monterey · Salinas · Fresno · Solvang · Los Angeles · Anaheim

0 75 150 miles
0 75 150 kilometers

Immigrants soon became a large part of the California workforce. Immigrants brought more than labor to California, however. They brought their kinds of music, dance, food, and celebrations. Immigrants have made California a richer and more diverse place to live. Japanese immigrant Kenju Ikuta showed that rice could be a California cash crop. As a result, many rice farms were started in Northern California. Gaetano Merola came to California from Italy in 1921. Two years later he started the San Francisco Opera.

Lesson from
Manzanar

An exhibit about something that happened in World War II can teach us something about tolerance today.

Corbis

U.S. ships at Pearl Harbor after the attack of December 7, 1941

On December 7, 1941, Japanese war planes bombed U.S. planes and ships at Pearl Harbor, Hawaii. The attack destroyed nine ships. It also destroyed 188 aircraft. More than 4,000 Americans were hurt or killed. The United States immediately entered World War II.

After Pearl Harbor, the United States believed that the Japanese were planning a larger attack. President Franklin Roosevelt worried that Japanese Americans might help the Japanese government. What if Japanese Americans in California were spies for the enemy?

President Roosevelt approved a plan he thought would protect the United States from Japanese spies. The plan gave army commanders the power to round up all Japanese and Japanese American people on the West Coast of the United States. All of these people, even those who were American citizens, had to leave or else live in internment camps, also called war relocation centers.

This is the notice that ordered Japanese and Japanese Americans to internment camps. ▶

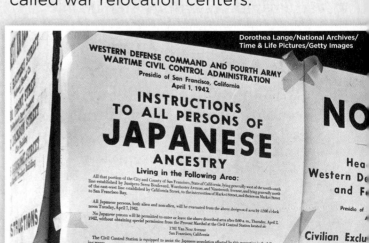

Dorothea Lange/National Archives/Time & Life Pictures/Getty Images

WESTERN DEFENSE COMMAND AND FOURTH ARMY
WARTIME CIVIL CONTROL ADMINISTRATION
Presidio of San Francisco, California
April 1, 1942

INSTRUCTIONS
TO ALL PERSONS OF
JAPANESE
ANCESTRY

Living in the Following Area:

TIME FOR KIDS

The entrance to Manzanar, with the barracks in the background

▲ **Families coped with crowded conditions and little privacy.**

At age 10, Mas Okui was sent with his father and two brothers to the Manzanar War Relocation Center. Manzanar was a Japanese internment camp. It was set on a windswept square-mile north of Los Angeles. For three years Okui lived in tar paper–covered barracks. For privacy, he had to string sheets between bunks.

Later, as a schoolteacher, Okui ran tours of the site. Now Okui and the 120,000 other people who lived in internment camps will have their stories told.

The National Park Service opened a center for visitors to Manzanar. There, people have the chance to learn about the internment of Japanese and Japanese Americans during the war.

The exhibit links the anti-Japanese feelings some people felt during World War II with the anti-Arab feelings some people felt after the 2001 attack on the World Trade Center. The purpose of the exhibit is to promote "dialogue on civil rights, democracy, and freedom."

Okui says, "What Manzanar should do is say to people, 'We did this. These people were cruelly treated. And I hope it never happens again.'"

▼ **This monument at the Manzanar cemetery has the words, "Monument for the Pacification of Spirits."**

Cause/Effect Writing Frame

Use the Writing Frame below to orally summarize "Land of Opportunity."

At the end of the 1800s, people came to California for **many reasons**.

One reason was to escape _____

_____ .

Another reason was _____

or jobs _____ .

The land, climate, and economic growth in California gave many

immigrants _____

_____ .

Other people made a living working in _____

_____ .

This explains why immigrants settled in _____

_____ .

Use the frame to write the summary on another sheet of paper.
Be sure to include the **bold** signal words. Keep this as a model of
this Text Structure.

Critical Thinking

1 A large movement of people from one place to another is known as _____ .

   A. immigration

   B. migration

   C. mutualistas

2 Point to the word in "Land of Opportunity" for hatred or unfair treatment of a particular group.

3 Locate the section in "Lesson from Manzanar" that explains why President Roosevelt approved internment camps.

4 Review the map on page 157 with a partner. Discuss the cities where many immigrant groups settled. Are more of these cities located on the coast or inland?

A key or legend helps you interpret the colors or special symbols on a map.

Digital Learning

For a list of links and activities that relate to this History/Social Science standard, visit the California Treasures Web site at www.macmillanmh.com to access the Content Readers resources. Have children visit the Field Trip "San Francisco's Chinatown."

THE RISE OF SOUTHERN CALIFORNIA

The population boom of the 1800s mainly affected the gold rich areas of Northern California. Southern California's boom was not far behind. Railroads, industry, oil, and Hollywood brought millions of newcomers. Between 1880 and 1920, the population of Los Angeles grew from 11,000 to over a half million.

One reason for the population boom was the discovery of oil, or "black gold." In 1893, Edward Doheny noticed that the back of a passing wagon was filled with sticky dark soil. Doheny and a partner bought the land and drilled down until they struck oil. Then they built an oil **derrick** above the source. A derrick is a tower built over a drill site to support a drill and bring oil to the surface. Soon people from around the country moved to Southern California to find oil and strike it rich.

At the same time railroads began using oil for fuel instead of coal. Cars powered by gasoline (an oil product) were becoming popular. For cars to use oil, the fuel needed to be **refined**, or improved. In the 1920s petroleum refining became California's biggest industry. More oil was exported from Los Angeles than from any other port in the world.

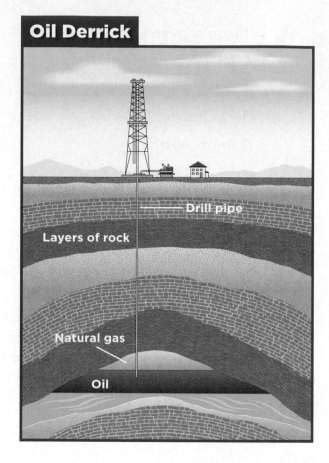

Oil Derrick

Drill pipe

Layers of rock

Natural gas

Oil

Los Angeles was not prepared for a population boom. It needed to be able to ship supplies in and products out. In 1907 the Port of Los Angeles opened. The port became the first stop in California for all ships coming from Europe, the eastern United States, and Central and South America. By the mid 1920s, Los Angeles was the busiest port in the western United States. The city was becoming an important new center of trade.

Because of the population boom, Los Angeles was outgrowing its water supply. In 1890 William Mulholland became head of the Los Angeles water department. Mulholland's solution was to build an **aqueduct** to bring water to the city. An aqueduct is a large pipe or other channel that carries water over a long distance. The Los Angeles Aqueduct ran from the Owens River to Los Angeles, a distance of 200 miles. It irrigated farms and supplied water to the people of Los Angeles. Meanwhile, without a river flowing into it any longer, Owens Lake dried up and Owens Valley farmlands suffered. By 1930 most of the farmers and ranchers in the Owens Valley sold their land and water rights to the city and rented the land back to ranchers.

Los Angeles Aqueduct

Legend:
- ▭ Los Angeles Aqueduct
- ○ Reservoir
- • City
- ▲ Mountain peak
- ⟲ Owens Lake (dry)

Lee Vining · Mono Lake · Crowley Lake · Pleasant Valley · SIERRA NEVADA · Big Pine · Owens R. · Tinemaha · Independence · Kings River · Mount Whitney ▲ · Haiwee · Fairmont · Bouquet · Palmdale · Los Angeles · Los Angeles · PACIFIC OCEAN

0   30   60 miles
0   30   60 kilometers

▼ **The Los Angeles Aqueduct opened on November 5, 1913.**

Two California Photographers

They captured the people and places of California during the first half of the 20th century.

Dorothea Lange

Dorothea Lange was born in Hoboken, New Jersey, in 1895. Lange learned photography in New York City. Later she moved to California to be a professional photographer.

In 1929 the Great Depression hit. Suddenly, many people did not have homes or jobs. Lange started taking pictures of poor people. One of the pictures she took, called *The Migrant Mother*, became very famous.

▲ Lange's *The Migrant Mother*

In 1940, Lange became the first woman to win an important prize for photography. During World War II, she photographed Japanese Americans who were imprisoned by the U.S. government.

Today Lange's work is well known. It is shown in museums around the world. *The Migrant Mother* was even turned into a postage stamp.

▼ Photograph by Lange of a Japanese family imprisoned by the U.S. during World War II

Ansel Adams

Ansel Adams was born in San Francisco in 1902. He studied to be a musician, but became interested in photography at a young age.

After a vacation with his family in Yosemite National Park when he was 14, Adams fell in love with the natural beauty there. He loved mountain climbing and was good at it. He began to develop his method of photographing natural landscapes.

Adams became interested in saving the wilderness. His photos showed national parks as they were before humans arrived. The photos were not only beautiful but they also helped to protect the natural world.

Adams also took pictures of people and buildings. During World War II, like Dorothea Lange, he took pictures of Japanese Americans imprisoned in internment camps such as Manzanar. He later worked with Lange on a series of photographs of a shipyard in Richmond, California.

Ansel Adams became one of America's best-loved photographers. He won many prizes, and his work is still shown around the world. —*Lisa Jo Rudy*

▲ Adams's *Moon and Half Dome*, Yosemite National Park

▼ **Photograph by Adams of a family in a Japanese internment camp**

Library of Congress

165

Compare/Contrast Writing Frame

Use the Writing Frame below to orally summarize "Two California Photographers."

Dorothea Lange and Ansel Adams were **similar** in many ways.

They were alike because they were _____.

In addition, **they both** lived _____.

In some ways, however, _____ and

_____ **were different**. Lange was born

_____,

while Adams _____.

Another difference was their work. Adams developed a method for

_____.

However during World War II, **both** photographers _____

_____.

They also worked together on _____

_____.

Use the frame to write the summary on another sheet of paper.
Be sure to include the **bold** signal words. Keep this as a model of
this Text Structure.

Critical Thinking

1 A large pipe that carries water over a long distance is a
_____.

   A. port

   B. derrick

   C. aqueduct

2 Locate the sentence in "The Rise of Southern California" that defines why oil needs to be refined.

3 Reread the paragraph in "Two California Photographers" that explains what happened when the Great Depression hit.

Diagrams provide information that may not appear in the text.

4 Look at the diagram on page 162. Discuss with a partner how the diagram supports the text.

Digital Learning

For a list of links and activities that relate to this History/Social Science standard, visit the California Treasures Web site at www.macmillanmh.com to access the Content Readers resources. Have children view the Biography "Ansel Adams."

OUR GOVERNMENT

The U.S. Constitution was written over 200 years ago. It explains the role of the **federal**, or national, government in our country. The Constitution says that the government has three branches, or parts. Each branch has its own job to do. Each branch also has some power over the other branches. This prevents any single branch from gaining too much power. The Constitution also limits the responsibility of the federal government by giving a lot of responsibility to each of our country's 50 states.

Branches of the Federal Government

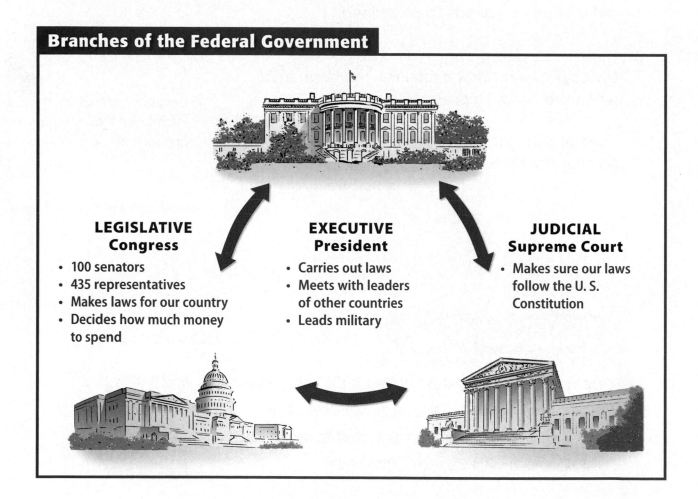

LEGISLATIVE
Congress

- 100 senators
- 435 representatives
- Makes laws for our country
- Decides how much money to spend

EXECUTIVE
President

- Carries out laws
- Meets with leaders of other countries
- Leads military

JUDICIAL
Supreme Court

- Makes sure our laws follow the U. S. Constitution

The **legislative branch**, or Congress, is the lawmaking part of government. It includes the Senate and the House of Representatives. Citizens elect senators and representatives to serve terms in Congress. Every state sends two senators to Congress. The number of representatives for each state depends on the state's population. The larger the state's population, the more representatives it has. California has 53 representatives, more than any other state.

Each year members of Congress meet in the Capitol to discuss issues and make new laws. They also help decide how the government will spend its money.

The **executive branch** carries out the laws. It is led by the President, who is also commander in chief of the U. S. military.

The **judicial branch** of the federal government includes all the federal courts. These courts make sure the laws are followed. The Supreme Court is the highest court in the country. It decides if new laws passed by Congress and approved by the President agree with the Constitution. In this way, the judicial branch limits the powers of the legislative and executive branches.

The California Constitution, written in 1849, was modeled on the U. S. Constitution. Both constitutions divide the government into three branches. Both have a written list of people's rights, such as the freedom of speech and religion. Over the years the California Constitution has been slightly modified.

The U. S. Constitution applies to all of the citizen of our country. The California Constitution applies only to Californians. Also, the California Constitution is longer. Sections of it explain in detail the specific responsibilities of the state government.

America's Grand Plan

On September 17 each year, the United States celebrates Constitution Day.

On September 17, 1787, 39 men put their names on one of history's most important documents: the Constitution of the United States of America. They had spent nearly four months in Philadelphia, Pennsylvania, discussing the best way to structure the federal government. Finally they signed the document that is to this day the master plan for how our government works.

NARA

▲ The Preamble of "America's grand plan"

The U.S. Constitution divides power between the legislative, judicial, and executive branches of the federal government. It also divides powers between the national and state governments. Some powers are specifically given to the federal government. All powers not given to the federal government are reserved for the states.

George Washington and others at the signing of the Constitution, September 17, 1787

Bettmann/Corbis

California's Constitution

The U.S. Constitution allows states to have their own constitutions. State constitutions allow states to take care of their own needs. California's constitution, for example, establishes a plan for the state's government and its education system. It gives the state a way to collect taxes and spend tax money. The California state constitution includes ways to protect the state's ocean resources.

▲ The seat of California's state government in Sacramento

A Reason to Celebrate

In 2004, President George W. Bush signed a law that officially established September 17 as Constitution Day. The law requires public schools across the country to devote time on September 17 to the Constitution. The first official celebration came in 2005. —*Martha Pickerill*

▲ Kids sign a copy of the Constitution at the National Constitution Center in Philadelphia.

Who Has the Power?

Here is a table of how the Constitution divides some powers between the two levels of government. There are powers that are for one level only and powers that are shared by the national and state governments.

Power	Is It a National Government Power?	Is It a State Government Power?
Print money	Yes	No
Declare war	Yes	No
Give out licenses	No	Yes
Create public schools	No	Yes
Collect taxes	Yes	Yes
Build roads	Yes	Yes
Make laws	Yes	Yes

Description Writing Frame

Use the Writing Frame below to orally summarize "Our Government."

The government has three branches, or parts. Each branch has its own job to do.

For example, the legislative branch, or Congress, _____

_____ .

It includes _____

_____ .

Another branch is _____ .

It is led by the President, who is also _____

_____ .

The judicial branch of the federal government includes all the

federal courts. **For example**, _____

_____ .

The _____ limits the powers of
the legislative and executive branches.

Use the frame to write the summary on another sheet of paper.
Be sure to include the **bold** signal words. Keep this as a model of
this Text Structure.

Critical Thinking

1 The _____ branch carries out the laws.

   A. executive

   B. judicial

   C. legislative

2 Find the sentence in "Our Government" that explains the word *federal*.

3 Point to the place in "America's Grand Plan" that gives an example of how the Constitution divides some powers between the two levels of government.

4 Review the diagram on page 168. With a partner, discuss how it helps you understand the text.

Diagrams are graphic aids that show how things relate to each other.

Digital Learning

For a list of links and activities that relate to this History/Social Science standard, visit the California Treasures Web site at www.macmillanmh.com to access the Content Readers resources. Have children view the Biography "Mariano Guadalupe Vallejo."

HOW STATE GOVERNMENT WORKS

California's government is located in Sacramento, the state's capital. Like the U. S. government, California's government has three branches. Members of the legislative and executive branches work in the state capitol building.

The state legislature consists of the 80-member State Assembly and the 40-member Senate. California citizens elect members of the Assembly for two-year terms and members of the Senate for four-year terms. Assembly members can serve up to three terms, and Senators up to two terms.

The U. S. and California legislatures debate and analyze **bills**. A bill is a suggestion for a new law. For example, in 1996, the state legislature debated a bill to decrease the size of many public elementary school classes. Although it would be a costly law to carry out, they voted in favor of the bill.

Once most of the members of the Assembly and the Senate vote in favor of a bill, it goes to the governor for approval. The governor is the head of the state's executive branch.

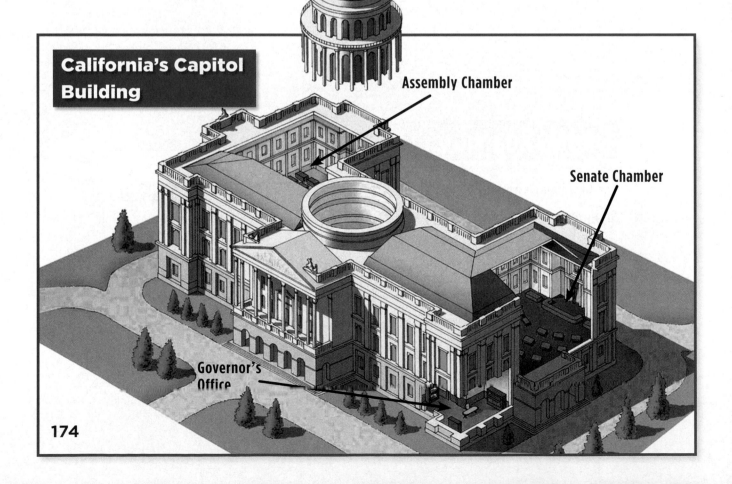

California's Capitol Building

Assembly Chamber

Senate Chamber

Governor's Office

California citizens elect governors to serve up to two four-year terms. The governor has the power to approve new laws by signing the bill. The governor can also **veto** the bill. A veto sends the bill back to the legislature.

The legislative branch then has the power to call a new vote on the bill. The bill will become a law if two thirds of the Assembly and Senate vote for it.

In 1996, Governor Pete Wilson signed the Class Size Reduction Program into law. It granted one billion dollars in the first year, and one billion dollars each year after that, to pay for more classrooms and teachers.

The judicial branch of the state government runs California's court system. It is similar to the federal judicial branch, except that it is responsible for upholding state law, not federal law.

The highest court in California is the California Supreme Court. The governor appoints each of its seven judges. Citizen then approve the judges in the next general election.

How a Bill Becomes a Law

1. Citizens develop an idea for a bill.

2. Members of the State Assembly or the Senate propose the bill.

3. The Assembly and the Senate vote to approve the bill.

yes   no ✓

4. The governor signs or vetoes the bill.

5. If the bill is vetoed, another vote can be taken. If more than two thirds of the Assembly and the Senate vote to approve it, the bill becomes a law.

Driver's License

A driver's license is more than just a license to drive.

A driver's license does more than just allow people to drive. In airports, at stores, and just about anywhere, a valid driver's license proves you are who you say you are.

Every state in the United States has its own laws about drivers' licenses. They are not all the same. All states do not have the same age requirements. For example in California and most other states, you have to be 18 to get a full operator's license.

Every state requires drivers to take a written test and a driving test. The written test includes questions about the rules of the road. The driving test asks new drivers to show that they can drive, back up, park, merge with traffic, obey traffic signs and signals, and react quickly.

Davd Young Wolff/PhotoEdit, Inc.

▲ Getting a driver's license is an important milestone for most teenagers.

Each state's license looks different, but they all have a photo and a special license number.

A National ID

Setting requirements for drivers' licenses—including ways of proving the identity of someone applying for a license—is the job of states. The U.S. government does not issue a national identification card the way many other countries do.

At airports and other secure places, though, the federal government requires people to prove who they are.

Blend Images/SuperStock

◀ All states require drivers to pass a driving test.

The U.S. accepts state-issued drivers' licenses as proof of identity. All states require applicants for drivers' licenses to prove their identity and age. This is usually done with a birth certificate, but other documents are also accepted. If an applicant comes from another country, a state employee may not have a way to make sure the information on documents provided is true.

Should requirements for drivers' licenses be made the same in all states? Should the federal government set standards for the kind of information applicants must provide? Congress may pass new laws that affect how states issue drivers' licenses. One change might be to require applicants to prove they are in the United States legally. Another could require states to store driver's license information in a database that other states could use. Would this make a driver's license a national ID card? If so, would that be a good thing or a bad thing? What do you think? —*Lisa Jo Rudy*

Many countries, including England, have a national ID card.

Joe Raedle/Getty Images

▼ **Driver's license applicants**

Sequence Writing Frame

Use the Writing Frame below to orally summarize "How State Government Works."

The first step in becoming a bill is _____

_____ .

Next _____

_____ .

Then _____

_____ .

After that _____

_____ .

If the bill is vetoed, **then** _____

_____ .

If more than two thirds of the Assembly and the Senate vote to

approve it, the bill **finally** _____ .

Use the frame to write the summary on another sheet of paper.
Be sure to include the **bold** signal words. Keep this as a model of
this Text Structure.

Critical Thinking

1 A _____ is a suggestion for a new law.

    A. veto

    B. bill

    C. assembly

2 Find the sentence in "Driver's License" that discusses the uses of a driver's license.

3 Should there be a national ID program in the United States? Point to one sentence in "Driver's License" that supports and one sentence that is against a national ID.

4 Review the diagram on page 174. Is the governor's office closer to the senate chamber or the assembly chamber? Discuss your answer with a partner.

Diagrams provide additional information that may not appear within the text.

Digital Learning

For a list of links and activities that relate to this History/Social Science standard, visit the California Treasures Web site at www.macmillanmh.com to access the Content Readers resources. Have children visit the Field Trip "Sacramento."

OUR LOCAL GOVERNMENT

Most cites and towns are governed by **city councils**. A city council is like the legislative branch of a city. It makes laws for the city. Most city councils have an odd number of members, usually five, seven, or nine. This is so when a vote is called, it will not end in a tie.

Council member are elected by citizens. In most California cities, the city council will usually hire a city manager to run the day-to-day affairs of the city. The city manager's job is to make sure all of the departments run smoothly. Look at the chart on this page to learn about the many departments of a local government and what they do.

In many cities, citizens elect a **mayor** to be the head of the local government. In San Francisco, for example, the mayor appoints, or picks, people to run city departments.

Most of California's cities are not as large as San Francisco. In many smaller cities, such as Chico, the mayor is not elected directly by voters. Instead the mayor is chosen by the city council from among its members. The mayor then serves as the head of the city council.

Every city and town in California is part of a larger **county**. A county is one of the sections into which a state is divided. California has 58 counties.

Department of Local Government

 Fire Department provides ambulance, fire, and rescue services

 Parks and Recreation Department maintains parks

 Planning Department plans for city projects

 Police Department keeps citizens safe

 Public Health Department helps citizens fight disease

 Building Inspection Department grants permits for new buildings, inspects plans

 Environmental Services Department oversees garbage, recycling

 Finance Department collects taxes, handles city money

 Maintenance Department repairs streets, signs, traffic lights

▲ Californians of all backgrounds benefit from public education.

Counties are governed by boards of supervisors. The board usually has five members, each of whom represents a different district in the county.

A county will provide many of the services of a local government. One important difference is that a county is responsible for hospitals and courts. Courts make up the judicial branch of a local government.

Another kind of local government is tribal government. There are over 100 Native American reservations and rancherias in California. Each has its own **tribal government**.

Like city governments, tribal governments are responsible for a wide range of services. They provide police, fire, and environmental protection. They operate schools, offer health care, and run job assistance programs.

Local governments do not always provide all the services people need. Sometimes a district is formed to manage a service that falls outside a local government's responsibility. There are over 2,000 special districts in California, each run by a board of directors. Special taxes pay for special districts. You are familiar with one service run by a special district—your school district.

California is divided into hundreds of school districts. Each district is run by a school board. The members of the school board work with the state's education department to make decisions about public education. California has the largest school system of any state in our nation. Nearly 6.5 million students attend public school in California.

In the Middle

Schools are working to find just the right spot for sixth graders.

Kennedy Frank likes being a sixth grader. "I have the privilege of changing classes," she told TFK. "And I'm getting new experiences by not having the same teacher all day." But she still takes comfort in being with old friends and seeing familiar teachers.

Kennedy, 11, goes to Humboldt Park K–8 School in Milwaukee, Wisconsin. *K–8* stands for "kindergarten through eighth grade." The school is part of a growing movement to change the way kids ages 10 through 15 are educated. More and more educators are turning away from middle schools for grades 6–8 in favor of K–8 schools. School districts from California to New York are opening more K–8 schools.

Kevin J. Miyazaki/Redux

▲ **In K-8 schools, younger kids can learn from older kids.**

Learning from the Past

Middle schools were created in the 1970s to fix problems in traditional junior high schools. Those schools housed grades 7–9. Middle schools were supposed to ease kids into the challenges of high school. They offered a curriculum tailored to fit kids' changing lives. Middle schools added sixth graders, to help ease overcrowding in elementary schools.

Recent studies suggest that middle schools aren't doing any better than junior highs were. Psychologist Jaana Juvonen says sixth grade is a poor time to switch schools. Kids' minds and bodies are going through a lot of changes at that age. They need "more stability in terms of relationships with teachers and their peers."

The move to middle school also seems to have an effect on classroom performance. Between 1999 and 2004 the nation's elementary school students scored higher on reading and math tests. Middle school students made smaller gains in math but no progress in reading.

▲ Young teenagers may need more stability than middle schools offer.

Still, some argue that test scores can't tell the whole story. Barry Fein, principal of Seth Low Intermediate School in New York City, believes in middle schools because they offer students more classes, team sports, and clubs. Ryan Pallas, a seventh grader at Las Flores Middle School, in Rancho Santa Margarita, California, agrees. "I like being challenged," he says. "It's more like real life."

No Easy Answers

In California, issues like these are decided at the level of local government, within individual school districts. In the Capistrano Unified School District, parents and students can choose either a K–8 school or a middle school. "K–8 isn't a [magic] bullet," says Lois Anderson, a Capistrano assistant superintendent. "It won't make other challenges go away."

What's the Difference?

K-8 | | MIDDLE SCHOOL

K–8		Middle School
▶ Many K–8 schools now offer labs, lockers, and other facilities similar to middle schools' in an environment that's familiar to sixth graders.	**Building Blocks**	▶ Middle schools tend to be larger and are often equipped with high-tech areas, including big libraries and science labs.
▶ Older students in K–8 schools are making solid gains in math and reading. Teachers and administrators tend to know more about students.	**Got Class?**	▶ Big middle schools have a richer selection of classes and more activities. Some states require that middle school teachers have special training.
▶ Older kids have a chance to be leaders for younger students. Sixth graders don't have the stress of a big move.	**Social Studies**	▶ New school, new friends. For some, it's a long-awaited fresh start. But others may not like being the youngest.

183

Problem/Solution Writing Frame

Use the Writing Frame below to orally summarize "In the Middle."

Many school districts are turning away from middle schools for grades 6–8 in favor of K–8 schools.

The problem is that _____

_____

_____ .

According to psychologist Jaana Juvonen, **this problem**

happened because _____

_____

_____ .

To help solve this problem many school districts are allowing

_____

_____

_____ .

Use the frame to write the summary on another sheet of paper. Be sure to include the **bold** signal words. Keep this as a model of this Text Structure.

Critical Thinking

1 A city council is like the _____ branch of a city.

   A. legislative

   B. executive

   C. judicial

2 Find the sentence in "Our Local Government" that explains tribal government.

3 Locate the section in "In the Middle" that describes the effect middle schools have on classroom performance.

4 Review the chart on page 183. Would you rather go to a middle school or a K–8 school? Discuss with a partner.

> A chart has columns and rows. Some charts are read down the columns, while the others are read across rows.

Digital Learning

For a list of links and activities that relate to this History/Social Science standard, visit the California Treasures Web site at www.macmillanmh.com to access the Content Readers resources. Have children view the Biography "Heather Fong."

Illustration Acknowledgements

7, 13: Argosy Publishing. 18: Tom Leonard. 30, 49, 60: Sam Tomasello. 162: Steve Stankiewicz. 168: Min Jae Hong. 174: Inklink. 175: Kenneth Batelman. 180: Rob Schuster

Photography Acknowledgements

All photos for Macmillan/McGraw-Hill except as noted below:

Cover: James Randklev/CORBIS. 6: Daryl Benson/Masterfile. 12: DK Limited/CORBIS. 13: BananaStock/PunchStock. 18: Siede Preis/Getty Images. 25: (tr) Yoav Levy/Phototake; (bcl) NASA JSC/Getty Images. 31: Phil Schermeister/CORBIS. 36: (b) Royalty-free/CORBIS; (br) Ian Rose/Frank Lane Picture Agency/CORBIS. 37: (cl) Joe McDonald/CORBIS; (bc) Steve Kaufman/Peter Arnold Inc.; (cr) Robert W. Ginn/PhotoEdit; (br) Eye of Science/Photo Researchers. 42: AGE Fotostock/SuperStock. 43: Robert Pickett/CORBIS; (br) Stockbyte. 54: (b) Frank Krahmer/Zefa/CORBIS; (inset) Frank Krahmer/Zefa/CORBIS. 55: (bl) Mervyn Rees/Alamy; (br) Anup Shah/Taxi/Getty Images; (b) Raymond Gehman/CORBIS. 60: Hans Pfletschinger/Peter Arnold Inc. 61: George D. Lepp/CORBIS. 66: Stephen Dalton/NHPA. 67: (tr) Kevin Schafer/CORBIS; (b) Klaus Nigge/NGS Images/Getty Images. 73: (cr) Roland Birke/Peter Arnold Inc.; (tcr) Custom Medical Stock Photo/Alamy; (br) PHOTOTAKE Inc./Alamy. 78: (t to b) TH Foto-Werbung/Photo Researchers; Wally Eberhart/Visuals Unlimited; Ben Johnson/Photo Researchers; Andy Crawford/DK Images; Randy Allbritton/Getty Images; Wally Eberhart/Visuals Unlimited; Image Farm Inc./Alamy; Lawrence Lawry/Photo Researchers. 79: (cr) Andrew J. Martinez/Photo Researchers; (br) Joyce Photographics/Photo Researchers; (b) Brad Lewis/Visuals Unlimited; (bl) Joyce Photographics/Photo Researchers; (cl) Creatas/PunchStock. 84: Royalty-free/CORBIS. 85: Carmel Studios/SuperStock. 90: (tr) Tony Arruza/CORBIS; (b) AGE Fotostock/SuperStock. 91: Joel W. Rogers/CORBIS. 108: (b) Gibson Stock Photography; (cr) Theo Allofs/Visuals Unlimited. 115: John Hudson/The Field Museum. 121: (b) Gary Crabbe/Enlightened Images; (tcr) Robert Holmes/CORBIS. 133: Brian A. Vikander/CORBIS. 138: Dave G. Houser/CORBIS. 144: Courtesy of the Bancroft Library, University of California, Berkeley. 145: Gary Moon. 156: Courtesy of State Museum Resource Center, California State Parks. 163: CORBIS. 181: Bill Aron/PhotoEdit Inc.